NOMOS
GLASHÜTTE

In support of

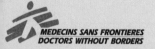

MEDECINS SANS FRONTIERES
DOCTORS WITHOUT BORDERS

Time for life—with limited edition timepieces in support of Doctors Without Borders/ Médecins Sans Frontières. Each watch raises 100 USD, GBP, or EUR for the Nobel Peace Prize winning humanitarian organization. And still these handcrafted mechanical watches with the red 12 cost the same as the classic models from NOMOS Glashütte. Help now, wear forever.

Funds raised are donated to Médecins Sans Frontières USA, UK, or Germany, depending on the specific model purchased. For MSF UK, the registered charity no. is 1026588. Available at selected retailers in the three participating countries, as well as online. Find your nearest NOMOS retailer at **nomos-glashuette.com** or order online at **nomos-store.com**.

GRANTA

12 Addison Avenue, London W11 4QR | email editorial@granta.com
To subscribe go to granta.com, or call 020 8955 7011 (free phone 0500 004 033)
in the United Kingdom, 845-267-3031 (toll-free 866-438-6150) in the United States

ISSUE 136: SUMMER 2016

PUBLISHER AND EDITOR	Sigrid Rausing
DEPUTY EDITOR	Rosalind Porter
ACTING DEPUTY EDITOR	Luke Brown
POETRY EDITOR	Rachael Allen
ONLINE EDITOR	Luke Neima
ASSISTANT EDITOR	Francisco Vilhena
DESIGNER	Daniela Silva
EDITORIAL ASSISTANTS	Eleanor Chandler, Josie Mitchell
SUBSCRIPTIONS	David Robinson
PUBLICITY	Pru Rowlandson
TO ADVERTISE CONTACT	Kate Rochester, katerochester@granta.com
FINANCE	Morgan Graver
SALES AND MARKETING	Iain Chapple, Katie Hayward
IT MANAGER	Mark Williams
PRODUCTION ASSOCIATE	Sarah Wasley
PROOFS	Katherine Fry, Jessica Kelly, Lesley Levene, Vimbai Shire
CONTRIBUTING EDITORS	Daniel Alarcón, Anne Carson, Mohsin Hamid, Isabel Hilton, Michael Hofmann, A.M. Homes, Janet Malcolm, Adam Nicolson, Edmund White

English National Ballet

AKRAM KHAN'S
GISELLE

A new interpretation of the iconic ballet

Manchester
Palace Theatre
27 Sep – 1 Oct

Bristol
The Bristol Hippodrome
18 – 22 Oct

Southampton
The Mayflower Theatre
26 – 29 Oct

London
Sadler's Wells
15 – 19 Nov

Book now **ballet.org.uk**

Co-produced by Manchester International Festival
and Sadler's Wells, London

Tamara Rojo and Akram Khan. Image © Laurent Liotardo

Creative
Writing
Online

Benefit from UEA's world renowned expertise and reputation. Online courses in prose and poetry available.

'I discovered a great deal about the process of writing and my own strengths and weaknesses'

'Everyone was so encouraging and polite. It was clear that people on the course were serious about writing'

'The tutor was superb'

New courses start October 2016
Register your interest at www.writerscentrenorwich.org.uk

WRITERS'
CENTRE
NORWICH

— National Centre *for* Writing —

University of East Anglia

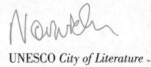

UNESCO *City of Literature*

literaturfestival.com

16.
internationales
literaturfestival berlin
7. – 17. September 2016

HAUPT STADT KULTUR FONDS

Zu Gast im Haus der
Berliner Festspiele

 Auswärtiges Amt

 FONDATION
JAN MICHALSKI
POUR
L'ÉCRITURE
ET LA
LITTÉRATURE

 HEINRICH BÖLL STIFTUNG

DECEMBER 7–10, 2016

NEW LITERATURE FROM EUROPE FESTIVAL

Full line-up announced September 1, 2016

For more information visit: www.newlitfromeurope.org

Curated and produced by 20 Square Feet Productions www.20squarefeet.com

Photos by Jack Llewellyn-Karski

Don't miss 15 of Europe's most exciting literary voices together with America's leading authors for conversations, performances, panel discussions, and readings at bookstores, cultural centers, libraries, and cafés across New York City.

The New Literature from Europe Festival is presented by:

Arts Council Malta in New York and
National Book Council (Malta)

Austrian Cultural Forum

Balassi Institute Hungarian
Cultural Center New York

Elizabeth Kostova Foundation

Goethe-Institut

Institut Ramon Llull

Literature Ireland

Polish Cultural Institute New York

Republic of Estonia Ministry of Culture

Romanian Cultural Institute New York

AMMOUN
VOYAGES

Moroccan Medinas

Ancient Numidia & Mauretania
with Prof David Mattingly (Algeria)

Gauguin in Brittany

Georgian Rtveli Festival
Vineyards & Monasteries

Memories & Magnolia
Literary trails of the Deep South (USA)

Sartiglia Masked Carnival (Sardinia)

The Birth of Frankenstein & "Vampyre"
Lac Léman winter weekend
(Switzerland)

Persian Shrines, Palaces & Ancient Cities (Iran)

www.ammounvoyages.co.uk

CONTENTS

Introduction

Emily Dickinson refers to two legacies in one of her poems; one of love and one of pain, the latter 'capacious as the sea'. Love and pain, love and loss: the two are twinned. To know love is to know (or to imagine) the loss of love.

In some cultures, of course, the risk of love is much greater than the potential loss of that love. In Nigeria, and in many other countries around the world, homosexuality is criminalised. Pwaangulongii Dauod's essay in this issue, 'Africa's Future Has No Space for Stupid Black Men', is about C. Boy, a student activist who formed a gay club to support LGBT people, some of whom were shunned by their families, and vulnerable to state persecution. Running such a club is a crime in Nigeria, punishable by up to ten years in prison. Homosexual cohabitation can lead to jail terms of up to fourteen years, and worse in the northern areas which have adopted sharia law.

Dauod's essay, sent to me by Binyavanga Wainaina, founding editor of Kenyan literary magazine *Kwani?*, shows the dangers of state-sponsored homophobia: fear, concealment, suicide. It also shows resistance. This essay is not only about homophobia – it is also about the relationship between individuals and the state, and a movement of hope and regeneration.

Each story in this issue is about love. Patrick Flanery writes about adoption: 'I find him in front of the painting. Though you can't tell much about the boy in the picture, he must be about the same age as the boy standing there on the carpet in the living room, the boy who is now, I remind myself, my son.' The boy is six, previously neglected and somewhat feral; he creates disorder in the aesthetic space and the well-ordered life. The painting Flanery refers to is by South African artist Kate Gottgens. It depicts a boy with a tied-on tail and an enigmatic smile, his pose watchful and energetic – you can see it on page 68. Flanery's story evokes the question of how love emerges when you adopt a child of that age, in the context of damage and transition between families, between cultures, and between neighbourhoods.

Like Erica Jong, the Danish writer Suzanne Brøgger wrote freely about sexuality and women's liberation. This extract from her diaries, translated by the author, is a time piece of the 1980s.

Brøgger is in love, but she is also stalked; the stalker does not accept her new relationship, and may love her, or perhaps he hates her. It's hard to know: the narrative of stalking hasn't settled yet.

Claire Hajaj tells the story of one of Syria's refugees in Lebanon. It's a true story, and one in which Claire and her husband were closely involved. Thanks to them, it ended well, but Hajaj's narrative is haunted by all the other stories, the refugees we walk away from without helping: 'They turn us into moral cowards; the more reasons they give us to stop, the faster we walk, and the tighter we cling to the belief that we have some useful, urgent destination.'

Love is haunted by loss; generosity is haunted by guilt.

K athleen Collins was an African-American film-maker, artist, educator and writer. We lead with the title story of her hitherto unpublished collection of stories, 'Whatever Happened to Interracial Love?'. The narrator is a young black woman, relatively privileged – she has been to college, the only black woman of her cohort at Sarah Lawrence; she is in love with a white civil rights activist, she lives on the Upper West Side, she hangs out with poets and community organisers.

'It's the year of "the human being"', Collins writes, ' The year of race-creed-color blindness. It's 1963.' She ironically identifies the race of each character in brackets and quotation marks: ('white'), or ('negro') – an oblique comment on the reality of that 'race-creed-color blindness'.

The author ends her story: 'It's 1963. Whatever happened to interracial love?'

It's 2016. Whatever did happen to interracial love, and to 'race-creed-color blindness'? ■

Sigrid Rausing

© LORNA SIMPSON
Black Cloud, 2011
from the *Ebony Collages* series
Courtesy of the artist and Salon 94, New York

WHATEVER HAPPENED TO INTERRACIAL LOVE?

Kathleen Collins

An apartment on the Upper West Side. Shared by two interracial roommates. It's the year of 'the human being'. The year of race-creed-color blindness. It's 1963. One roommate ('white') is a Harlem community organizer, working out of a storefront on Lenox Avenue. She is twenty-two and fresh out of Sarah Lawrence. She is twenty-two and in love with a young Umbra poet (among whom in later life such great names as Imamu Baraka and Ishmael Reed will be counted the most illustrious members). The other roommate ('negro') has just surfaced from the jail cells of Albany, Georgia. She is twenty-one and the only 'negro' in her graduating class. She is in love with a young, defiant freedom rider ('white') who has just had his jaw dislocated in a Mississippi jail. He is sitting with her at the breakfast table, his mouth wired for sound.

Among those who pass in and out of this interracial mecca: a photographer ('negro') who in a desperate moment just rifled their typewriter and headed towards the nearest pawnshop; a young, vital heroin addict ('negro') off the streets of Harlem whose constant companion is the nubile Sarah Lawrence girl ('white'); the Umbra poet ('negro') who is drinking coffee in the front room and reading a verse called 'June Bug!'; an assortment of bright-eyed women ('white') fresh from a prayer vigil on the steps of our nation's Capitol;

a few rebellious-looking women ('negro') en route to Itta Bena, Mississippi, to renounce their Northern bourgeois heritage. Idealism came back in style. People got along for a while. Inside the melting pot. Inside the melting pot.

It's summer. The 'negro' roommate and her young 'white' lover are considering marriage. In a while, she'll take him to the hospital to meet her father (a stroke victim from an overdose of idealism). In a while, her short white lover with the overhung lip (so that he stuttered slightly) will confront the gray-haired distinction of New Jersey's first 'colored' principal. ('I love you,' he said . . . her lover, that is . . . 'I want to be a Negro for you,' he said . . .) Her father will fix his deep gray bourgeois eyes on her and not move a muscle.

It's summer. The Sarah Lawrence graduate is listening to her Umbra poet. He is dark and quiet, and his eyes dart back and forth across her face while he reads. The apartment is growing dusky (*and* dusty). Later the coterie will prepare to attend a rent-strike meeting in Harlem, or a fundraising benefit for SNCC, or a voter registration meeting in Newark, New Jersey.

We are in the year of racial, religious, and ethnic mildew. 'Negro' families in Montclair, New Jersey; Brookfield, Massachusetts; Hartford, Connecticut; Mount Vernon, New York; Washington, DC – the hidden enclaves of the *Black Bourgeoisie* (a book that will be taken down from the dusty shelves of some obscure small-town library and soon issued in paperback, causing the fortunes of an obscure 'negro' sociologist to rise) – will see their children abandon a lifetime of de-ghettoizing. Their sons will go to jail for freedom (which in their parents' minds is no different than going to jail for armed robbery, heroin addiction, pimping, and other assorted ethnic hustles). Their daughters will kneel in prayer on the dusty red-clay roads of Georgia, as if the neat velvet pews of the Episcopal Church had never been their first encounter with religion. The 'First Coloreds' in medicine, law, politics, baseball, education, engineering, basketball, biochemical research, the armed services, tennis and film production will all be asked to come forward and speak about their success. Ralph Bunche will become a household name. Everyone who is anyone will find at least one 'negro' to bring along home for dinner. It's the year of 'the human being'. It's 1963: whatever happened to interracial love?

In our Upper West Side apartment our young ('negro') roommate has just come back from the hospital with her freedom rider. She is ashamed and strangely depressed. The bleak look in her father's eyes was not reassuring. He could not move a muscle, yet he seemed to be saying, 'Is it for *this* that I fought and struggled all these years, for *this*, *this* indecent commingling?' He does not seem to understand the shape of the world to come. He does not seem to understand that this young, colored woman he has spawned does not, herself, believe in color: that to her the young freedom rider of her dreams is colorless (as indeed he is), that their feelings begin where color ends (as indeed they must), that if only he could understand that race as an issue, race as a social factor, race as a political or economic stumbling block, race is part of the past. Can't he see that love is color-free? She is close to tears. The gray, bourgeois eyes remain fixed in her mind.

Her lover sits dejectedly in the sunless room (when they took the apartment, she chose the back bedroom just off the foyer, thinking it would provide her greater privacy. It does, but it is also without light and by the end of her time there she will discover that almost all her unhappiness stemmed from that dark and dusky corridor she called her room. It was only sunlight she needed. Pure, delicious sunlight flooding through a room). He is thinking about his parents, about his stern Bostonian upbringing. His father will not even venture to meet the girl he has chosen to marry. His mother will only agree to a secret rendezvous in some out-of-the-way Boston restaurant. How can he bring his father to an understanding of what it feels like to be beaten to a pulp? Teeth mashed in, jaw dislocated, nose rearranged, stomach pulpy. And all for freedom. All for the 'negroes' of this land we call America. It is imperative that his father understand that he has not been betrayed, that he, the son, is in fact trying to fulfill the father's dream, that dream that he, the father, believes in deep, deep down. Somewhere way deep down. He, the son. It's 1963: we're in the year of prophetic fulfillment. The last revival meeting is at hand, where the sons took up the cross of the fathers. White sons went forth to the dirt roads of Georgia and Alabama to prove to their fathers that the melting pot could still melt. 'Negro' sons went forth to the Woolworths and Grants and Greyhounds of America to prove to their fathers that they could eat and sit and ride as well in the front as in the back, as well seated as standing.

Her lover sits in the sunless room feeling dejected. Soon he is to return to the cotton fields for some more 'grassroots organizing'. His Boston accent flirts with the edges of a Southern drawl. His white face floats in a sea of black protest. It is a time that calls forth the most picturesque of metaphors, for we are swimming along in the mythical underbelly of America . . . there where it is soft and prickly, where you may rub your nose against the grainy sands of illusion and come up bleeding.

O ur young lover ('white'), upon his return, will land in jail a second time, where he will refuse to post bail, refuse to eat, refuse to keep his mouth shut until he is again beaten into irrational silence, his mouth once more wired for sound. His father does not come to his aid. His mother begs him to use the enclosed check and come home. His ('negro') lady writes him poetic letters from her Upper West Side apartment with here and there a little Emily Dickinson for encouragement ('I'm Nobody! Who are you?') and a little Edna St Vincent Millay when a more elegiac mood reigns ('if I should learn in some quite casual way that you were gone, never to return again'). They will pass the winter in this desultory fashion.

T he ('negro') roommate takes refuge in her sunless room. In the face of her father's paralytic sternness, in the face of her lover's imprisonment, she sits, sips tea, and relives the 'negro' void of her college years (what was it like to be *the only one*????).

She recalls her father's freshman admonition on how to avoid the roommate problem (EEEEK!!!! There's a 'negro' in my room!!!): always request a single. She remembers each one of those singles – one for every year. Though she was never lonely. They made her class president (for freshman openers), then honor board representative (for sophomore encores), then class-something-or-other the year after that . . . she was sure she was one of them, until that fateful day THE SIT-INS STARTED and she began to wonder why, in fact, she was so privileged when, according to THE SIT-INNERS (who came in droves to lecture at every near-white institution in the country), many of the members of her race (they were still a long way away from being 'her people') were living in poverty and despair, deprived even of the right to vote, a basic American right. Yet they were Americans, just as she herself was an American. So at Easter time she announced to her father (who had not yet had his stroke) that she would be going South that summer to work as a voter registration worker, that she would be going South that summer to find out once and for all what it was like to be a 'negro'.

And that summer had brought her one startling and overwhelming realization: that she could marry *anyone,* not just a colored doctor-dentist-lawyer-educator, but *anyone*: a Mexican truck driver. A Japanese psychiatrist. A South African journalist. Anyone. Up to and including a white man. This was the ripest fruit from a summer spent picking cotton and cucumbers, and taking sun baths in Mama Dolly's chicken yard with another 'negro' friend who was also escaping her bourgeois past. They were turning themselves into earth women, black (the word surfaces!) women of the soil, in harmony with the ebb and flow of nature, in harmony with the Southern earth of their ancestry, and the deep Southern sky, and the moody Southern stars.

It was there that she met her young lover ('white') who shared their bare existence of cornbread and chitterlings, while together they combed the hot dirt roads pleading with folks to come out and vote, come out and be shot, come out and lay down their life on the interracial line. She had an ear for public speaking. She attributed this to some Southern ancestry deeply ignored by her parents (and never let it occur to her that her father before his paralytic crisis was himself a most persuasive speaker). She loved standing in the pulpit with outstretched arms, tears rolling down her cheeks, offering herself to freedom and begging others to join her, join this great hand-holding, we-shall-overcome bandwagon of interraciality when black and white would, in fact, walk hand in hand to freedom.

A shiver curved down her spine. She sat still in the sunless room and remembered. The fear. That she had pushed somewhere out of reach. That she had refused to acknowledge, until the day they shot holes all through Mama Dolly's farm and she came home. To her last year of school. To make speeches, and sing songs, and raise money. But never, ever to go back. Not even when the leader of the Movement himself begged her to use her college degree and come back and teach. She would make speeches and sing and raise money and send clothes. But never go back. Except through the eyes of her lover ('white') who lay awake nights in that same Mississippi jail. That was the closest she ever came to a return.

She closes her eyes for a moment. She is reading: *The Rise and Fall of the Third Reich*; *Toward a Psychology of Being*; *Rabbit, Run*; *The Centaur* ('Listen to me, lady. I love you, I want to be a Negro for you . . .'). And every Wednesday at five o'clock she sat for an hour and unburdened herself on a very sleepy psychiatrist whose continual dozing was a sure sign that not only was *she* boring, but that any life dissected too closely was boring and could only make you fall asleep. He diagnosed her as manic depressive. All negroes were prone to manic depression, he told her. They were all subject to frenzied highs, followed by sudden, depressive lows, he told her. It must have to do with all that singing and dancing, he told her. So she went to the library and looked up manic depressive, to catalogue her symptoms and hang them on her wall: prone to ecstatic moments followed by severe depressions with accompanying loss of self-esteem, feelings of meaninglessness, and a sense of the insignificance of life (later she would laugh when she discovered that meaninglessness came from the dark shaft of gloom that surrounded her day and night and that ecstasy was just a sunny room away).

She wished her father would forgive her lapses. Her racial ones as well as her sexual ones. After her first night in bed, she was astonished: *that* was what the fuss was all about? *That* was why her father watched over her with lock and key, scrutinizing every date as a potential enemy? For *that*?? That peculiar slipping and sliding that occasionally provided a momentary gasp, a strange, slight convulsion? And then what? How could her father think she was going to the dogs because she had slept with one man and was about to marry another one ('white', true)? And what of it? She wished her father could talk, that he didn't just lay there and stare at her, like she was really 'colored', like now she had really turned into 'a colored woman' and was beyond salvation. That was the real bug. Not that she had 'opened the doors to herself', as her mother put it, but that she had ceased to be her father's adored child. She had even committed the final sin, the unforgivable final sin of ('negro') girlhood: she had cut her hair. 'How few "negro" girls are blessed with long hair?' Her father had sobbed. 'How could you go and turn yourself into a negro just like any other negro? How could you do that?' And he turned and walked away. She could feel her skin turning darker while he lay there and stared at her; her hair felt not only short but unbelievably bushy. At any moment a toothless grin would spread across her face and she would be a walking replica of all of his nightmares – she would shuffle backwards and grin and her bushy hair would stand on end and she would have turned into 'a colored woman'. That was what she read in those gray bourgeois eyes; that was what caused the stroke: the sudden transformation of his beloved, intelligent daughter (she *was* the only 'negro' to graduate from that Alpine fortress) into 'a colored woman'. Such thoughts left her sticky and glued to her seat. If only she could abolish the gloom and let herself blossom under the light of this interracial love affair. If nothing else they would have beautiful children. They always were, these interracial urchins produced out of Chinese and white fusion, or Indian and negro fusion, or for that matter, white and negro fusion; as if through the process of mating the children took the best of all the features: added a little kink to the too-straight white hair, chiseled into aquiline the too-broad negro nose, rounded the tight, slinky Chinese eyes to a delicate almond shape. She liked thinking about a little interracial baby of her own. She put her hand on her stomach, and opened her eyes. The room was dark. Even with two 150 watt bulbs, the room was dark. She heard her roommate open the door.

Her roommate was a healthy-looking girl (whose name was Charlotte, by the way): the kind of girl who adored a lovable sheepdog at the age of three, and rode horses bareback at five; the kind of girl who was bred, not raised. And it showed, particularly around the eyes, and the deep healthy glow of the skin. It showed. With a trace of interracial rebellion in every strand of that vibrant, blonde hair.

If her roommate was healthy-looking, she, by comparison, was a bit anemic-looking. She was, for instance, too pale for a 'negro', with something a bit too yellow around the gills. Four years in the North woods of academia had given her very little opportunity to dress chicly as ('negro') women notoriously do, with a flair for the right place to hang a scarf, cock a hat, don a cacophony of colors with an uncanny, unerring taste for making it work. She had no such flair. Had, in fact, no flair whatsoever. If you thought of any color at all beside her, it was brown. That monotonous brown that goes well with a pair of Buster Brown shoes. Her first lover ('negro') had attempted some improvements on her looks. He had suggested, for example, that she eliminate that brushstroke of bright orange smeared inaccurately across her lips, that she stop those clumsy efforts at tweezing her thick, bushy eyebrows that were, in fact, her best feature. Suggested, in sum, that she stop trying to do something with herself, but instead just wear turtleneck sweaters (preferably black ones to go with her Buster Brown shoes), and one plain, corduroy skirt with big pockets.

Which she did. Even after they broke up (he took a motorcycle and headed out west with a new ('white') girlfriend).

Her roommate is reminding her that there is a poetry reading tonight down at St Marks on the Bowery and would she like to go with them? It's an Umbra reading. She's trying to decide when the key turns again in the lock and Henry ('negro'), the poet, enters. They are actually living *à trois* and sometimes *à quatre* when what's-his-face takes a brief furlough from jail. Right now there are only three of them. Henry is unquestionably endearing. With the softest voice you ever heard. Charlotte (her roommate) is considering supporting him for life. He could write poetry, she could work. It is not a particularly political dream – Henry is not about to go South and sit in, he is not even interested in voter registration, and his poems are curiously apolitical. It is really a romance, which will eventually pop (if one is willing to admit that romances are a bit like balloons). Charlotte found she didn't like working. Even for poetry. Henry read about her wedding in the *New York Times* (Sunday section). But we are light years away from this eventual outcome.

It's 1963. The windows to this ground-floor interracial mecca are always wide open. An assortment of people avoid the door and come in through the windows. There's Adrienne ('white'), another long-haired beauty of the Sarah Lawrence variety. She spends all her time with Skip, the ghetto youth with the heroin problem. She and Charlotte spend hours trying to devise ways to help Skip kick the habit and become a full-time rent-strike organizer with the other part of his time taken up with solving his daily problem. They see him as a beautiful human being 'caught in the currents of a segregated existence'; they fervently believe that their own infiltration of his lifestyle, their own willingness to live among him (and *with* him, if the need arises) will surely change all this. Integration is a pulsating new beat, which will liberate him from the old, segregated ways of doing things. For is it not, after all, *we*, who must overcome? WE, who must walk hand in hand? For if you (Skip) are not free, then it follows, as night follows day (an exquisite metaphor for our purpose), that I (Adrienne) am not free. Togetherness came back in style. People got along for a while. Inside the melting pot.

There is a tall, somber young man (West Indian, and West Indians are not 'negroes'), called Derek, who always rings the bell and waits politely to be admitted. He sits in the corner of Charlotte's room (all the congregating takes place in Charlotte's room which faces the street and the light and the ... we could go on) and pontificates. In his methodical, messianic mind there is a theory building that perhaps integration is just another form of imitation, that perhaps integration is just another form of stultification, that perhaps integration is just another form of impersonation, that perhaps ... and a year later he will shout from the podium, 'Black Power! Black Power! Black Power!' and the romance will go up in smoke (if one is willing to admit that romances are a bit like smoldering fires).

There is another quiet, diligent soul who frequents this integrated coterie. A prophetic soul who is looked upon as the Father of the Movement. He comes only to persuade everyone that they should use their education in the service of the massive voter education program he is starting in Mississippi. Its aim: to increase the literacy rate of Southerners ('negroes') and prepare them for political activity. He calls it the politics of arithmetic. He has understood that politics is the source of power and that Southern arithmetic (ten negroes + one white = eleven whites) should be reversed. It is a stunningly correct analysis that will go down in defeat at the Democratic Convention of 1964, when that illustrious body turns its back on the New Math. The sands of illusion are prickly and wet, and our Prophet will seek a final answer in the Fatherland, as all true prophets must. There is no honor in one's own apartment.

And what of love, instead of politics? What of that nubile, fleeting sensation, when one is color-blind, religion-blind, name, age, aid, vital statistics-blind? What about the love of two 'human beings', who mate, in spite of or because of or instead of or after the fact of? What of Henry and Charlotte and their possibilities for an integrated cast of children? What of all those interracial couples peppering the Lower East Side in the summer of '63 and the summer of '64 only to go into furtive decline in the summer of '65 – no longer to be seen holding hands in public ('Black Power! Black Power! Black Power!')?

But it's 1963 and Cheryl (we have neglected to name her) declines tonight's Umbra festivities. She is tired from reading *The Rise and Fall of the Third Reich; Toward a Psychology of Being; Rabbit, Run;* and *The Centaur* ('Listen to me, lady. I love you, I want to be a Negro for you . . .'). She will not go with Charlotte and Henry, even though Henry is reading 'June Bug!', her favorite poem. She will stay home and practice her stream-of-consciousness therapy, isolating herself in her closet (the only place in her room where her desk fits) and writing automatically, putting down everything that comes into her head (. . . my father sat me down on his lap when Mrs Drexel slapped me and he told me not to worry about that old librarian slapping me just because I asked if we could take a break and she looked at me like I was a troublemaker and slapped me across the face and the shoe man gave me a pair of tasteless shoes and the brightest red lipstick he had and I insisted loudly that the shoes were in bad taste and lipstick was too gaudy because I didn't wear shoes like that just because I was colored and couldn't he tell I didn't give off any odor of any kind just because I was colored and that I always held my breath every time I went into his store because I was colored and didn't want to give off any odor of any kind so I tightened my stomach muscles and stopped breathing and that way I knew that nothing unpleasant would escape – not a thought nor an odor nor an ungrammatical sentence nor bad posture nor halitosis nor pimples because I was sucking in my stomach and holding it while I tried on his shoes and couldn't he see that I was one of those colored people who had taste). The book said that if you did this every night for an hour, you could speed up the analytical process, and maybe cure your own self and Cheryl was very anxious to be cured of her manic depression at a cheaper rate than twenty-five bucks an hour so she sat in the deep gloom of her room and wrote and wrote and refused to think or punctuate or let her mind do anything but record every single syllable that popped into her head. Censored thoughts were passing out of her unconscious at an amazing rate. Afterwards she couldn't lift her wrist from the desk or decipher one syllable. But she was sure she was making progress.

This was always the last performance of the night. Before bedtime. Then she turned out the light and let her thoughts take her to that Mississippi jail cell. Where Alan (as he was prosaically named) rotted. She would compare their sexual coupling ('black' and 'white' together) to her first encounter. Did he (Alan) seem smaller simply because she was trying to overcome three hundred years of mythological white impotence in order to mate healthily with him? Or was he smaller? It was a difficult thing to determine. If he *was* smaller, then surely race played no part in it. It was just coincidence that Aaron (the first time they made love it was on the Staten Island ferry) –

We were very tired, we were very merry—
We had gone back and forth all night on the ferry

– was bigger. Race was not a factor. Sexual fulfillment was color-blind. And she tried to put herself to sleep but couldn't. She began thinking about Charlotte, whom she admired a great deal. There was something incredibly attractive about her healthy, bold looks. She would have liked to have Charlotte's boldness. Her face had a frankness that held your attention.

They had met at a Civil Rights conference at Sarah Lawrence a year before Charlotte's graduation. Charlotte had come to New York first (Cheryl didn't graduate until the following year) but whenever Cheryl came to New York for the weekend, she stayed at Charlotte's apartment. They agreed to take an apartment together after Cheryl's graduation. Charlotte was sexually ripe. Beside her Cheryl felt like a novice. It wasn't that they ever talked about sex. They didn't. They talked about babies a lot though, about what beautiful babies she and

Henry would have if they had babies. Charlotte's eyes would look almost dazed with pleasure. But Cheryl was always vaguely irritated by Charlotte and Henry's relationship. In her eyes Henry was too meek. Perhaps because she liked noisy, more vociferous men. Perhaps not. Perhaps Henry was just meek. But his meekness irritated her. She found it subservient. And she disliked him for it. He never got angry, never raised his voice above a whisper, spent all his time in Charlotte's room writing while Charlotte spent all her time in Harlem in a storefront office organizing rent strikes. That didn't seem right.

Once, Cheryl's mother and father came to dinner and Henry was there too. They all ate in the kitchen at the small round table and her father's eyes kept filling up with tears. He could not reconcile his daughter to this place. He could not reconcile his daughter to Charlotte (with all her frank breeding spilling all over the place), not to Charlotte and Henry (with all their frank sexuality spilling all over the place). When Cheryl accompanied them to their car, he was still crying. He asked her to come home, he realized now that he had made a terrible mistake sending her to that exclusive school to be the first and only one. It had made her queer. It had made her want a queer life among queer, unnatural people. It was not what he had in mind at all. He had simply wanted her to have a good education with a solid respected ('white') name behind it. That was all he had wanted. Then he had expected her to come home again and teach and get married and live in the apartment on their third floor. He did not want her to lead this queer integrated life with some pasty freedom rider who liked to flagellate himself for ('negroes'). It was unhealthy. It was wrong. He should go home, too. They should all go home. Henry should go back to his ghetto. Charlotte should return to her well-bred country life. She, Cheryl, should come home and get a job teaching school. Everything else was too queer, too unspeakably queer and made him cry.

It was not a successful dinner party. Cheryl felt depressed and hid in her closet to try a little automatic writing (Daddy you must see that I must lead my own life even if you don't understand it and all this talk about color all the time I'm not the same anymore and I have to be what I am I've lived with all kinds of people even if they were all white and now I'm trying to live with some white people and some 'negro' people and find out who I am and I have to do it and . . .). And then the doorbell rang. Strange. It was past midnight. And she was alone. Henry and Charlotte were still down at another Umbra reading. She peeked cautiously through the keyhole. It was Alan. Out of jail. Standing in the doorway. And crying. No, no, don't touch. He said, no, please. He had something to say: he had just come from his parents' house. He knew now that he could not marry her. He knew now that he would never go back South. It was over. He had come to say goodbye. It was all over. He understood now that he could never be 'a negro'. Never. Ever. And then he was gone.

She went into her room and sat down. She opened *The Rise and Fall of the Third Reich*. But she couldn't see. Then opened *The Centaur.* 'Listen to me, lady. I love you, I want to be a Negro for you . . . But I cannot, quite. I cannot quite make that scene. A final membrane restrains me. I am my father's son . . .' She had never read the ending. She did not know that was how it ended. She had thought it was possible to rupture every membrane and begin at zero.

Then she thought. I must find an apartment high up, around the twentieth floor, where the sun will come flooding in in the morning and I won't awaken inside a deep shaft of gloom. Then I will be able to think and see clearly, about how integration came into style. And people getting along for a while. Inside the melting pot. Inside the melting pot.

It's 1963. Whatever happened to interracial love? ∎

Hoa Nguyen

Stripes on My Shirt Like Migratory Birds

'I got lost in my life'
which may or may not be

misheard
Drink a cheap Canadian 'wine sparkler'

& kvetch about _____

& read an article on the six-
minute brain-delay built-in

        Bought store-bought white
organic bread   ('You ruin everything'

those ghosts said)   and also
foil packets of Vitamin C   A spring

white wine even though it calls
for snow: April 10, 2016 (Toronto)

Did really challenge white
feminist hegemony?

Roasted fennel bulbs

Killed a pink potted mum
           accidentally

ARCADIA

Emma Cline

'There's room for expansion,' Otto said over breakfast, reading the thin-paged free newspaper the organic people sent out to all the farms. He tapped an article with his thick finger, and Peter noticed that Otto's nail was colored black with nail polish, or a marker. Or maybe it was only a blood blister.

'We draw a leaf or some shit on our label,' Otto said, squinting at the page. 'Even if it just kind of looks like this. People wouldn't know the difference.'

Heddy simmered slices of lemon at the stove, poking at the pan with a chopstick. She'd changed into a sweater dress and her legs were rashy. Every morning since she found out she was pregnant, she'd been drinking hot lemon water. 'It corrects your pH levels,' she'd explained to Peter. She used the hot water to wash down all her prenatal vitamins, big dun-colored pills that smelled like fish food, pills that promised to soak the baby in minerals and proteins. It was strange for Peter to imagine their baby's fingernails hardening inside her, its muscles uncoiling. The unbelievable lozenge of its heart.

Heddy pursed her lips sideways at her brother. 'That's kind of stupid, isn't it?' she said. 'I mean, why don't we just get certified, the real way?'

Otto fluttered his hand. 'Got a few thousand lying around? You're certainly not contributing.'

'I'm broadening my mind.' She was starting her first semester at the junior college in town.

'You know what broadens after that?' Otto said. 'Your ass.'

'Fuck you.'

'Yeah, yeah. I had to hire more people and that costs.'

Peter had seen these new workers: a bearded man and a woman, who'd moved into one of the trailers a few weeks ago. They had a young boy with them.

'It all costs,' Otto said.

Heddy narrowed her eyes but turned back to the pan, intent on fishing out the lemon.

'Anyway,' Otto continued, 'we can still say "natural" and all the rest.'

'Sounds good,' Peter said, trying to be enthusiastic. Otto was already shuffling the pages, on to something new. He seemed to like Peter as much as he liked anyone. When he found out that Peter had gotten Heddy pregnant, it was his idea that Peter move in and work for him. 'I guess she's eighteen,' Otto had said. 'No longer my worry. But if I see so much as a bruise, I'll end you.'

Heddy put her hand on Peter's shoulder: 'He's teasing,' she said.

Peter had moved into Heddy's childhood bedroom, still cluttered with her porcelain dolls and crumbling prom corsages, and tried to ignore the fact of Otto's room just down the hall. Otto managed the hundred and fifty acres of orchard surrounding the house. The land was near enough to the North Coast that great schooners of fog soaked the mornings with silent snow. When it rained, the creek outran its banks, a muddy, frigid surge that swamped the rows of apple trees. Peter preferred it up here, the thousand shades of gray and green instead of Fresno with the sameness of heat and dust.

By the time he and Otto had finished breakfast – eggs from the chickens, fried in oil and too salty – Heddy had gone up to their bedroom and come down with all her things, her raincoat already zipped, a canvas backpack over her shoulder. He knew she'd already packed it with notebooks, a separate one for each class, and her chunky cubes of Post-its. No doubt she'd devised a color-coded system for her pens.

Otto kissed her goodbye, making a lazy swat at her ass as he headed out to turn the heater on in the truck, leaving Heddy and Peter alone in the kitchen.

'Heddy's off to Yale,' she announced. She tightened her raincoat hood and grinned at him from the circle within. With her face isolated by the hood, she looked about twelve, the blooms of color on her cheeks tilting even more cartoonish. She slept through most everything – the dogs, the rooster, thunderstorms – and it seemed like proof of her greater moral center, something Peter could imagine existing as whole and real in her as a red apple. An innocence coupled with a strange knowingness: when they had sex, she kept looking down to watch him go inside her.

'You look pretty,' Peter said. 'Done at four, right?'

Heddy nodded. 'Home around five,' she said. She loosened her hood, pulling it back to expose her hair, the tracks from her comb still visible.

Peter and Otto spent the day in near silence, the seats of Otto's truck giving off vapors of leather. Otto drove the orchard roads, stopping only so Peter could dash out in the rain to open a gate, or chase down the ripple of an empty candy wrapper. No matter how much time they spent together, Peter couldn't shake a nervousness around Otto, a wary formality. People liked Otto, thought he was fun. And he was fun, the brittle kind of fun that could easily sour. Peter hadn't ever seen Otto do anything, but he'd seen the ghosts of his anger. The first week Peter had moved in, he'd come across a hole punched in the kitchen wall. Heddy only rolled her eyes and said, 'He sometimes drinks too much.' She said the same thing when they saw the crumpled tail light on the truck. Peter tried to get serious and even brought up his own father, dredging up one of the tamer stories, but Heddy stopped him. 'Otto pretty much raised me,' she said. Peter knew their mother moved to the East Coast with her second husband,

and their father had died when Heddy was fourteen. 'He's just having his shithead fun.'

And they did love each other, Otto and Heddy, living in easy parallel habitation, as if the other person was a given, beyond like or dislike. They surprised Peter sometimes with their sentimentality. Some nights, they watched the movies they'd loved as children, colorized films from the fifties and sixties: orphans who could talk to animals, a family of musicians that lived in a submarine. The movies were oddly innocent – they bored Peter, but Otto and Heddy loved them without irony. Otto's face went strangely soft during these movies, Heddy on the couch between Otto and Peter, her socked feet escaping from under the blanket. Peter heard them talking, sometimes: they carried on long, sober conversations, their voices sounding strangely adult, conversations that trailed off whenever Peter came into the room. He'd been surprised that neither Heddy nor Otto cared that much about nudity, Otto striding naked down the hall to the shower, his chest latticed with dark hair.

When Peter talked to Otto, it was only about yield. How many tons of almonds per acre, what kind of applications they'd make to the soil in a few weeks, after harvest was over. When they drove past any of the workers in their blue rain ponchos, up in the trees on ladders, or gathered around chubby orange water coolers, Otto would honk the horn so they jumped. One man held up his hand in silent greeting. Others shielded their eyes to watch the truck pass.

They were mostly seasonal pickers, moving from farm to farm, and a few students on leave from fancy colleges. The students accepted produce and a place to live as trade, an arrangement that Otto found endlessly amusing. 'They got college degrees!' Otto crowed. 'They email these fucking essays to me. Like I'm going to turn them down.'

The new guy Otto had hired was different. Otto didn't even ask him if he'd work for trade. He had already asked for advances on his salary, accompanied by careful lists of his hours written on the backs of envelopes. Peter knew Otto had let the guy's wife work, too.

Nobody seemed to care who watched their boy, except for Peter, who kept his mouth shut.

A round noon, Otto pulled the truck off into a grove of stony oaks. They left the doors of the truck open, Peter with a paper bag between his knees: a sandwich Heddy had made for him the night before, a rock-hard pear. Otto produced a bag of deli meat and a slice of white bread.

'The kid from Boston asks if he can take pictures while he harvests,' Otto said, folding a slice of meat into the bread. 'What for? I ask him.' Otto paused to chew, then swallowed loudly. 'For his website, he says to me.' He rolled his eyes.

'We should get a website,' Peter said, unwrapping the pear. 'It's not a bad idea.'

It had actually been Heddy's idea. She'd written about it in her notebook. Heddy's notebook wasn't expressly secret, but Peter knew he wasn't supposed to read it. It was for her self-improvement. She wrote down business ideas for the farm. Kept itemized lists of the food she ate, along with calorie counts. Wrote down what days of the week she would wear her teeth-whitening strips, what days she would jog around the orchards, ideas for baby names. She'd written the beginnings of bad, sentimental songs that confused him, songs about pockets full of rain, men with no faces. One page she'd filled with his name, over and over in ballpoint pen. It took on a new life, his name, repeated like that. The inane embroidery.

'A website,' Otto said, stuffing the ham into his mouth. 'Freeman Farms on the Web. Get one of the college kids to do the thing. With photos. Apples you'd want to fuck.'

Otto laughed at his own joke. Under the far grove of trees, Peter could see the workers, clustered together for their lunch. Since it had stopped raining, some of them had hung their dripping ponchos in the branches, for shade.

O tto and Peter spent the rest of the afternoon in the office. Otto had Peter handle the phone calls to their accounts. 'You sound nicer,' he said. After Peter finished up a call with the co-op in Beaverton, Otto jabbed a chewed-up pen in his direction.

'Go find out who's gonna make our website,' he said. 'I want flashy shit, too, blinking lights and video and everything.' He paused. 'Maybe a place for a picture of us, too. So people can see who they're doing business with.'

'That's a good idea.'

'It makes people feel safe,' Otto said. 'Doesn't it? To see a face.'

H eddy had taken his car to school, so Peter drove Otto's truck out to the trailers, the passenger seat full of the cartons of extra eggs from the chickens. The workers lived in five aluminum-sided mobile homes, the roofs tangled with wires and satellite dishes, yards cruddy with bicycles and a broken moped. He could tell which cars belonged to the college kids, who needed even their vehicles to be blatant with opinions: they were the cars scaled with bumper stickers. Otto had let the college kids pour a concrete slab by the road a few months ago; now there was a brick grill and a basketball hoop, and even a small garden, scorched and full of weeds.

As he approached, Peter saw a boy out in front of the first trailer, the boy from the new family, bouncing a mostly deflated ball off the concrete. He must have been eleven or twelve, and he stopped playing to watch Peter's truck approach. There was a shadow on the boy's shaved scalp; as Peter pulled up to the trailer, he realized it was a kind of scab or a burn, black with dried blood, thin and delicately crackled. It covered a patch of the boy's head like a jaunty cap.

A woman – the boy's mother, Peter assumed – opened the door of the trailer and stood on the concrete-block stoop, not closing the door fully behind her. She was in slippers and men's pants, cinched at the waist with a belt, and a ribbed tank top. She was younger than he would have guessed.

'Hi,' Peter said, stepping out of the car. He ran his fingers through his hair. It made him uncomfortable whenever Otto sent him to talk to the workers. Peter was twenty, the same age as some of the college kids. It wasn't so bad talking to them. But the real workers, the older men – Peter didn't like giving orders to them. Men who looked like his father; their red-rimmed eyes, the hunch of the manual laborer. Peter had harvested garlic in Gilroy during high school summers, had driven in the morning dark with his father, the cab stinking of the magenta grease they used on their Felcos. He remembered the way the group went quiet when they saw the foreman's truck, how it was only after the truck had fully retreated that they turned the radio up again, like even the meager pleasure of listening to music was something that had to be hidden.

'Otto said we could finish at three,' the woman said, picking at her shirt hem. She was kind of pretty, Peter saw as he walked over to her: long black hair she'd braided, the blurry edge of a badly done tattoo creeping over her shoulder. She reminded him of the girls in Fresno. 'It's after three,' she said.

'I know,' Peter said, sensing her worry. 'It's fine. Otto just wanted to know if someone knew about computers. Like, how to make websites. I'm supposed to ask around.'

'I know computers,' the boy said, picking up the ball. The ball was marbled in a trashy pale pink, and the boy pressed it between his hands so the ball bulged.

'Zack, baby,' the woman said. 'He doesn't mean you.'

'I know a lot,' Zack said, ignoring his mother.

Peter didn't know what to say. The kid seemed sick or something, his eyes unfocused. 'Otto wants a website for the farm,' Peter said, glancing from Zack to the woman. 'I'm Peter, by the way,' he said, holding out his hand.

The woman let the door shut behind her, walked over and shook his hand. 'I'm Steph,' she said. She seemed to get shy then. She put her hands on her son's thin shoulders. 'Matt's my husband,' she said. 'The beard?'

'Otto likes him a lot.'

'Matt works hard,' Steph said, brushing lint off Zack's T-shirt. 'He's at the store.'

'Does he know anything about computers?'

Zack said, 'Matt's dumb.'

'We don't say that, baby,' Steph said. She shot Peter a look, gauging his expression, then tried to smile. 'Matt's not great with computers. One of the younger people might be better,' she said, nodding her head at the trailers with the hammocks strung up in the yard.

'I'll ask them,' Peter said. 'Oh,' he remembered, 'I have eggs for you.' He walked back to the car and got a carton from the passenger seat. 'From the chickens,' he said.

Steph frowned. It took Peter a moment to understand.

'Just extras,' Peter said. 'It's not payment or anything.'

Steph smiled then, taking the carton, and shrugged. 'Thanks,' she said. The tattoo on her shoulder was a kind of vine, Peter saw as she came closer, thick and studded with black leaves. Or maybe they were thorns.

Zack let the ball drop to the concrete and reached out for the eggs. Steph shook her head at him, softly. 'They'll break, honey,' she said. 'It's best if I hold them.'

Zack kicked the ball hard, and Steph flinched when it hit the metal siding of the trailer.

Peter backed away. 'I'm just going next door,' he said, waving at Steph. 'It was good to meet you.'

'Sure,' Steph said, cradling the eggs to her chest. 'Say goodbye, Zack.'

Steph couldn't see, like Peter could, how Zack's face had tightened, a look of concentration fleeting across his face. Zack let one hand rise up to graze the edge of his wound. He scratched, and a quick filament of blood streamed down his forehead.

'He's bleeding,' Peter said, 'Jesus.' Steph let out a harsh breath of air.

'Shit,' she said, 'shit,' and she huddled Zack in her other arm, still clutching the eggs, and started pulling him toward the house. 'Inside,' she ordered, 'now. Thank you,' she called over her shoulder to Peter, struggling to get Zack up the steps, 'Thanks a ton,' and then the two of them disappeared inside, the door snapping shut.

Heddy came home breathless from her day; kisses on both of Peter's cheeks, her bags tossed on the counter. She used the office computer to look up a video on the Internet that showed her how to cover her books using paper shopping bags, then spent half an hour at her bedroom desk, dreamily filling in the name of each class, smudging the pencil with her fingertips.

'That's the only way to get a realistic shading,' Heddy explained. 'Like it?' she asked Peter, holding up a book.

'It's great,' Peter said, naked on top of the bed covers, and Heddy's eyes scatted down to study her drawing again. He had planned to tell her about his day, about Steph and Zack. That horrible wound. But it would make her sad, he thought, and she cried so easily now. Worried even when she had a bad dream, as if the fear would pass through her blood somehow and affect the baby.

'*Le Français*,' Heddy said, slowly. 'I got to pick a new name,' she said. 'For class. I'm Sylvie,' she said. 'Isn't that pretty?'

'It's nice,' Peter said.

'I got to pick second from a list. The girls who had to pick last got, like, Babette.' She erased something with great concentration, then blew the remnants away. 'I have to get special shoes,' she continued, 'for salsa class.'

'Salsa class?' Peter sat up to look at her. 'That's a class?'

'I need a physical education credit,' she said. She smiled a mysterious smile. 'Dancing. Good to know, for our wedding.'

He shifted. He wished suddenly that he was wearing underwear. 'Who do you dance with in this class?'

Heddy looked at him. 'My classmates. Is that okay?'

'I don't want some asshole bothering you.'

She laughed. 'God, Peter. I'm pregnant. Think I'm safe.'

He decided not to tell her about Steph and Zack.

'We're going to make a website for the farm,' Peter announced, lying back against the pillows.

'That's great,' she said. He waited for her to say more. To say it was her idea, not his. He sat up and saw she was still bent over her books.

'A website,' he repeated, louder. 'One of the workers knows how to make one. He can set it up so people can order off it.'

'That's wonderful,' she said, finally smiling at him. 'I've always thought we should have one.'

'Well,' he said, 'I had to convince Otto. But everyone else has one. It makes sense.'

'Exactly,' she said. She left her books on the desk to come to the bed, to lay her head on his chest. Her scalp was pure and clean through her parting. Her weight against him felt nice, the press of her tight belly, and he kissed the top of her head, her hair that held the cold of the air outside and smelled like nothing at all.

Peter propped the front door open with a brick and lugged cardboard boxes of canned food and plastic bags of bananas from the car to the kitchen table. He'd been in charge of grocery runs since Heddy started school. Rainfall was the heaviest it had been in twenty years, everything outside crusty with wet rot, and on the way to the house Peter stepped over a neon earthworm in the wet grass. The worm was slim, the color of bright new blood.

Peter cleaned out the refrigerator before putting the groceries away, throwing out the expired tub of baby spinach he'd bought on the last run, the leaves matted into a wet stink. He was still learning how to buy the right amount of food.

He could hear Otto moving around in the office. Otto had been working with one of the college kids to build the farm website. They had figured out the domain name, and there were some photos up already, a form to submit orders that was almost finished. The college kid spent a lot of time out on the porch, talking on his cell phone, his fingers pinched girlishly around a cigarette.

Peter watched now as the college kid walked back to the trailers through the gray rain. In the distance, greasy smoke was rising from the brick grill. He thought of Steph. Peter had seen her a few times, working alongside a man he assumed was Matt. She hadn't acknowledged him. Peter hadn't seen Zack outside the trailer again, even on sunny days.

Peter bought a notebook for himself on the grocery run. He'd meant to write in it, like Heddy did. Record his ideas, his thoughts about the world. He splayed it across his knees and waited with a pencil, a glass of water. But there was nothing he wanted to say. He wrote down what Otto had told him about living well on an acre, what plants to buy. What trees could grow from cuttings. What sort of drainage you'd need. He would need to know these things when he and Heddy got their own place. He let himself imagine it: no trailers crudding up the property. No Otto leaving commas of pubic hair on the toilet seat. Just him and Heddy and the baby. He put the notebook aside. The water in his glass had gone stale. He picked an apple from the bowl on the table and flicked open his pocket knife, making idle cuts in the apple's skin. It would be hours before Heddy came home.

Soon he started carving designs, words. It pleased him to get better at it, to let whole sections drop cleanly under his knife. He carved his own name over and over in loops he linked around the core. Liking the reveal of wet flesh against the red skin. He lined up the finished apples in the refrigerator, where the rotting spinach had been.

He napped on the couch and dreamt about Heddy dropping a glass, the two of them watching it explode blue and low on the ground. He jerked awake. It was dark already. Otto came into the kitchen and flicked on the light. He opened the refrigerator and burst out laughing.

'You are losing your mind.'

Peter looked up from the damp couch. Otto swung two apples by their stems, Peter's cuts withered and browning, wrinkled at what had been their sharp edges.

'Do you work only with apples? Or is there room for expansion?

I'm talking oranges here, pears,' Otto said. 'I'm so proud you're keeping busy.'

Peter got up when he heard the car outside. His shirt was wrinkled but he tucked it in as best he could.

'It's freezing,' Heddy said, hurrying through the door without a coat on. Her hair was dripping onto her shoulders, her raincoat bunched in her arms.

'Look,' she said. She held out the raincoat. 'Mold,' she said, flinging it to the floor. 'Crazy, huh?'

She didn't wait for Peter to answer.

'I'll have to get a new one,' she said, kissing him quickly. She tasted like chlorine. She'd started swimming after class in the school exercise center. 'Low-impact exercise,' she called it. She said it was good for the baby. Peter tried not to think about her body exposed to strangers in her swimsuit with the high-cut legs. How the seat of her swimsuit sometimes wedged itself into her ass. She got home later and later these days.

'How was swimming?'

'Fine,' Heddy said. Her hair was dripping all over the floor and she didn't seem to notice.

'You've always sucked at swimming,' Otto said to Heddy. He tore one of the plastic bags of bananas open with his teeth. He tried to peel a banana, but just mushed the top. Heddy reached over and grabbed the banana from Otto.

'It's easier to open it from the bottom,' she said, pinching the banana at its stubby end so the peel split cleanly under her fingers.

Otto narrowed his eyes at her, snatching the banana back. 'Thanks, genius,' he said. 'Glad to know you're learning so much. *Voulez-vous coucher avec moi* and all that shit.' He laughed, then turned to Peter. 'Sam fixed the home page,' he said. 'All the pictures load now.'

'Good,' Peter said. 'I told the co-op they could start ordering online in a week or so. They seemed happy.'

Heddy ignored both of them, kicking her raincoat in the direction of the trash can. Peter watched her while Otto kept talking. Each time she parked on campus, it cost ten dollars, and Peter knew she kept meaning to buy the parking pass that would save her a hundred bucks. Last week she told him, finally, that the pass was no longer a good deal. She seemed to feel this had been a great failure on her part, the failure to buy the parking pass in time.

Heddy set water to boil for her tea, cleaning her fingernails with the nails of her other hand, and then arranged herself at the table to do her homework. She'd gotten a bad grade on her first French test, and had seemed perplexed and hurt ever since. Peter didn't know how to help her.

Otto was telling Peter some story about one of the workers, some RV they wanted to park on the property.

'And I tell him, sure, be my guest, if you can even drive that thing,' Otto said.

'Can you guys go outside?' Heddy said, finally looking up at them. 'Sorry,' she said. 'I just – I have to call someone for school. On the phone.'

It was cold on the porch, the air gusting with the smell of wet earth. Peter hunched into his coat. Otto was still talking, but Peter wasn't listening. He looked up at the sky but couldn't orient himself. When he tried to focus, the stars oscillated into a single gaseous shimmer and he felt dizzy. Even on the porch he could hear Heddy inside on the phone. She was speaking halting French to someone she called Babette, and she kept breaking into English to correct herself. He felt ashamed for suspecting anything else.

'I know,' Heddy said. 'She is *très mal.*' Her accent was clumsy, and he felt bad for noticing. Through the windows, Peter saw her pacing the kitchen, her familiar shape made foreign by the pocked glass.

Otto paused his monologue to study Peter.

'Where's your head at, brother?' Otto said. 'You look like you're off in space.'

Peter shrugged. 'I'm right here.'

Inside, Heddy said a final '*Bonne nuit*'. Peter watched as she gathered her books and headed up the stairs, her shoulders a little hunched. Her rear was getting bigger, a humble sag that moved him. She turned out the lights as she left, like she forgot anyone was even out there.

Peter had thought it was coyotes, the whooping that woke him up. He stood at the window of their bedroom, feeling the cool air beyond the glass. The ragged calls filtered through the dark trees and had that coyote quality of revelry – his father used to say that coyotes sounded like teenagers having a party, and it was true. He hadn't spoken to his father since he'd left. But Peter had Heddy now. A house of their own that they'd live in with their baby, the curtains for the nursery that she'd want to sew herself.

The idea pleased him, and he glanced over. Heddy was still sleeping peacefully, her mouth open. The salts she liked to dissolve in her baths were still in the air, and a dark stain spread across the comforter from her wet hair. There was something new in her face, though, some cast of resignation, since the bad grade in French. At least she was still going to classes. She made a face when he'd asked about registration for next semester, as if even that was uncertain, though classes would end a month before her due date.

A dog had been killed a while ago; Heddy swore it had been a coyote, so Peter knew he would have to go downstairs to make sure the three dogs were tied up, that they hadn't left any of their food uneaten. He pulled his boots from under the bed and found his hat. Heddy turned over but didn't wake up.

The dogs were fine, up on their hind legs when they heard Peter coming. They whined and pulled their chains, dragging them heavily on the ground.

'You hear the coyotes?' he asked them. Their food bowls were empty and silver, smelling of their breath. 'You scared?'

The noise came again, and Peter stiffened. The coyotes were so human-sounding. He whooped back, crazily.

'Ha,' he said, scratching the dogs. 'I'm scary too.'

But the noises doubled then, and Peter could make out, in the mass of the cries, what sounded like whole words. He could see, far off in the orchard, car headlights turn on abruptly on one of the dirt roads, casting a smoldering wash of light on the surrounding land.

'Fuck.' Peter looked around. Otto's truck was gone; he was probably in town. Peter hurried to his own truck and started the ignition, then jumped out to untie one of the dogs, an Australian Shepherd that Heddy had named, to Otto's disgust, Snowy.

'Up,' he said, and Snowy leapt into the cab.

Heddy had taken the truck to school, and it smelled like wet clothes and cigarettes, the radio turned up full blast to the staticky dregs of the country station. She hadn't told him she'd started smoking again. Peter knew she wasn't supposed to smoke – pregnant women couldn't smoke. But suddenly he wasn't sure. Because Heddy wouldn't smoke if it could hurt the baby, he told himself. So maybe he had it wrong. Peter fumbled with the volume knob, turning the radio off, and took the ranch roads as fast as he could without headlights.

The strange headlights he had seen were still on, but the car wasn't moving. As Peter got closer, he slowed the truck, but he knew whoever it was had heard him. His heart beat fast in his chest, and he kept one hand on the dog.

Peter was close enough that his own truck was lit now. He parked and felt around under the seat until his hand closed around a short piece of broken rebar. 'Hello?' Peter called from the truck. The headlights of the other vehicle hummed steadily, and specks of bugs swooped in and out of the twin columns of light.

Peter climbed out of the truck, the dog following.

'Hello?' he repeated.

It took him a moment to understand that the other truck was familiar. And before he had understood it fully, Otto walked out from the darkness into the bright room made by the headlights.

He was drunker than Peter had ever seen him. He wasn't wearing a shirt. He looked to the air around Peter's face, smiling. Like an athlete in the stadium lights.

'Peter,' Otto said. 'You're here.'

Behind him, Peter saw two women giggling in the orchard. He could see that one was naked, a plastic camera on a strap around her wrist. He noticed the other woman's T-shirt and see-through lavender underwear before realizing, in a sickening moment, that it was Steph, her dark hair sticking to her face.

'Steph and I made a friend,' Otto slurred. 'Come on,' he said to Steph and the woman, impatient. 'Hurry up.'

The women held on to each other and stepped gingerly through the grass toward the trucks, the woman with the camera plumper than Steph. They were both wearing sneakers and socks.

'I know you,' said Steph, pointing at him. She was drunk, but it must have been something else besides alcohol. She couldn't quite focus on Peter, and she smiled in a strange, fanatic way.

'Hi,' said the plump girl. Her hair was blonde and worn long with jagged edges. 'I'm Kelly. I've never been to a farm before.'

Steph hugged Kelly, her small tipped breasts pressing into Kelly's larger ones. She said loudly into Kelly's ear, 'That's Peter.'

Otto kept licking his lips and trying to catch Peter's eyes, but Peter couldn't look at him. Snowy ran up to the women and they both shrieked. Steph kicked at the dog with her dirty tennis shoes as he tried to nose her crotch.

'Don't kill 'em,' Otto said to Snowy. 'I like 'em.'

'Come on, dog,' Peter said, patting his leg.

'You aren't going, are you?' Otto leaned against his truck. 'Help me finish this,' he said, the bottle in his hand sloshing.

'Don't go, Peter,' Steph said.

'I told them they'd only drink the best,' Otto said. He held out a bottle of grocery-store champagne to Peter. 'Open it for the girls.'

The bottle was warm. Snowy was agitated now, circling Peter's feet, and when Peter twisted the cork and it shot into the dark, Snowy yelped and took off after it. Steph took the bottle from Peter, the bubbles cascading down her arms and frothing into the hem of her underwear. Kelly clicked the shutter.

'See?' Otto said. 'That was easy.'

'Steph,' Peter said. 'Why don't I drive you back to your house, okay?'

Steph took a long drink from the bottle. She regarded Peter. Then she let her mouth drop open, bubbles and liquid falling down her front. She laughed.

'You're a disgusting girl,' Otto said. Snowy came to sniff at his boots, and Otto gave him a heavy kick. The dog whimpered. 'A disgusting girl,' Otto repeated.

'Hey, shut up,' Kelly said, meekly.

'Fuck you,' Otto said, smiling hard. 'Fuck. You.'

Peter started to move toward his own truck, but Otto came over and pushed him back, one hand steady on his chest.

'Come here,' Otto said to Steph, his hand still on Peter. 'Come on.'

Steph turned her back on Otto, pouting. Her buttocks through the netted underwear were shapeless and crisscrossed with impressions of the ground.

'Oh fuck off,' Otto said. 'Come here.'

Steph laughed, then took shaky steps toward Otto. He caught her and shoved his mouth against hers. When they pulled apart, he clapped at her ass. 'Okay, now kiss him.'

Peter shook his head. 'No.'

Otto was smiling and holding Steph by the hips. 'Kiss him, babe. Go on.'

Steph leaned over so her chapped lips brushed Peter's cheek, her body pressed against his arm. The shutter clicked before Peter could back away.

'Listen,' Peter said. 'Why don't you guys go somewhere else?'

'Really?' Otto laughed. 'Go somewhere else. Interesting suggestion.'

Peter hesitated. 'Just for tonight.'

'I own this fucking property. You are on my property right now.'

'Otto, go home. This isn't good.'

'Good? Don't you work for me? Don't you live in my house? You fuck my sister. I have to hear that shit.' He pushed Steph away. 'You think you know her? Do you even realize how long Heddy and I lived out here alone? Years,' he spat, 'for fucking *years*.'

Heddy was still asleep when Peter came into the bedroom, the room navy in the dark. He took off his clothes and got in bed beside her. His own heartbeat kept him awake. The house was too quiet, the mirror on Heddy's childhood vanity reflecting a silver knife of moonlight. Could a place work on you like an illness? That time when it rained and all the roads flooded – they'd been stuck on the farm for two days. You couldn't raise a baby in a place like this. A place where you could be trapped. His throat was tight. After a while, Heddy's eyes shuddered open, like his hurtling thoughts had been somehow audible. She blinked at him like a cat.

'Stop staring at me,' she said.

He tried to put his arm around her, but she'd closed her eyes again, nestling away from him, her feet soothing each other under the sheets.

'We need to get our own place.'

His voice sounded harsher than he'd meant it to, and her eyes startled open. She started to sit up, and he saw the shadowed outline of her bare breasts before she groped for the blankets and pulled them tight around her. It struck Peter, sadly, that she was covering her breasts from him.

He took a breath. 'I could get another job. You could be closer to school.'

She said nothing, staring down at the covers, pinching at the fake satin border.

He suddenly felt like crying. 'Don't you like school?' he said, his voice starting to unravel.

There was a silence before she spoke. 'I can just work here. For Otto.' She started to turn from him. 'And where am I ever going to speak French anyway?' she said. 'You think we'll take the baby to Paris?' She laughed, but it was airless, and Peter saw the tired hunch of her shoulders and understood that they would never leave.

The next morning, Peter woke to an empty room. Heddy's pillow was smoothed into blankness, the sun outside coming weak through the fog. From the window, he could see the dog circling under the shaggy, emerald trees and the trailers beyond. He forced himself to get up, moving like someone in a dream, barely aware of directing his limbs into his clothes. When he went downstairs, he found Otto on the couch, his shoes still on, fumy with alcohol sweat. A pastel quilt was pushed into a corner, and the couch pillows were on the ground. Otto started to sit up when Peter walked past. In the kitchen, Heddy had the tap running, filling the kettle.

'And on the couch, you'll notice my dear brother,' Heddy said, raising her eyebrows at Peter. There was nothing in her voice that indicated they'd talked the night before, just a faint tiredness in her face. She shut off the faucet. 'He smells like shit.'

'Morning, Peter,' Otto said, coming into the kitchen. Peter worked to keep his gaze steady and level on the tabletop as Otto pulled up a chair.

Heddy padded toward the stairs with her mug of lemon water, glancing back at them. Otto watched her go, then went to the sink and filled a glass with water. He drank it down, then drank another.

'I'm in hell,' Otto said.

Peter didn't say anything. A band of pressure built around his temple, a headache coming on.

Otto drank more water in huge gulps, then opened the cupboard. 'Do you forgive me?'

'Sure.'

Otto closed the cupboard without taking anything out. He turned to look at Peter, then shook his head, smiling. 'Shit. "Sure," he says. Listen,' Otto continued. 'I'm meeting these guys today who've been emailing. They want to work. You have to meet them too.'

The headache was going to be a bad one, a ghosted shimmer of the overhead light starting to edge into Peter's vision. 'I don't think I can,' he said.

'Oh, I think you can.' Otto said.

Peter couldn't speak, so Otto went on. 'So we'll meet here. Or do you want me to tell them we'll meet in town?'

Peter pulled at his collar, then let his hand drop. 'I guess town,' he said.

'Easy,' Otto said. 'Wasn't that easy?'

They finished their breakfast in silence. The room got soggy with quiet, the air pressing in, a stale vapor that seemed a hundred years old. Heddy stooped to kiss Peter goodbye, her bag over her shoulder. Peter forced himself to smile, to kiss her back.

'Lovebirds,' Otto called, and Peter looked over, just as Otto held up his hands to frame Heddy and Peter.

Heddy stood and Peter noticed she had put on slashes of dark eyeliner that made the whites of her eyes brighter. The faint smell of cigarettes lingered in the air where she had just been. Her hair was pinned up off her neck. She had on a light jacket instead of her old raincoat. She looked like a new person, like no one he knew. ∎

Vahni Capildeo

Is Fraid I Fraid Calendars

Listen, the day you reached
into the car compartment
for the house keys and didn't
find them, only jumbie beads
I'd collected out running,
and we checked, and panicked,
and pulling up outside
our then apparent house,
checked again for the keys
and there they were, easily:
that unsafe stashed miracle
was when some kind of physics
crossed one road into another.
Haven't you noticed people
are different since then? some worse;
others, distant; and a crop
of long-lost cousins, glistening
with the universe they know
and in which we share history,
insists on intending good?
Old Lady who talks tideline –
Old Man who thinks spiders –
Is fraid I fraid calendars,
the set of days on the door.

POTTED MEAT

Steven Dunn

Draw

Every day after me and Grandad sit on the porch and eat fried green tomatoes, my cousin teaches me how to draw. He makes dashed lines in the shapes of skyscrapers, men with gold chains, girls with big breasts. I connect the dashes until the picture is complete. My cousin tells me to get a new sheet of paper and draw what I just traced. I do. He says, You need to work on your buildings but you draw some good titties.

Grandma is in the living room. She usually smells like cottage cheese. But today she smells like chitlins. I eat so much vinegar with my chitlins my lips turn white. Grandma lights a long cigarette and stabs herself in the stomach with needles. She says it's insulin. She listens to a gospel song and sings, I'm coming up on the rough side of the mountain. My cousin says, She plays that goddamn song every day. She does. I like it. I ignore him and keep drawing titties.

The next day after me and Grandad sit on the porch and eat fried green tomatoes, my cousin gives me another lesson. He makes dashed lines in the shapes of a man with a knife, a woman in a bathtub, a keyhole. I don't want to trace these shapes. He grabs my hand and makes me. He tells me to get a new sheet of paper and draw what I just traced. I don't. He grabs my hand again. He says, You need to work on your stab wounds.

I run through the house crying. I want to tell Grandma but she's stabbing herself in the stomach. I run outside and tell Grandad. He stops playing cards with his friends and takes me in the garden. Here, he says, have a little wine. I need to tell you something, Grandad explains. When your cousin was five he saw some shit that messed him up. So dont worry too much about it, he been drawing that shit for years. Grandad tells his friends, Card game canceled – gotta fry some tomatoes for my boy here. See you suckas tomorrow, and dont forget my goddamn money, nigga.

My cousin is an artist. He says, You draw some good knives but you still need to work on your stab wounds. Lemme get one of them tomatoes. Check out my new Air Jordans. You need to learn how to rap. She plays that goddamn song every day.

Color

In class I sit behind Rhonda. She always raises her hand. I get to stare at her arm. I kick the back of her seat so she can turn around. I can look at the side of her face. I keep going to the pencil sharpener in the front so I can look at her eyes when I walk back.

I draw two pictures the same. One for me, one for Rhonda. I draw us holding hands in front of a house. Out of the chimney comes smoke shaped like hearts. A big puffy apple tree beside the house. On the tree is a heart with our initials. I start to color. Rhonda first. Hair yellow. Skin peach. I give Rhonda the picture. She smiles.

I run up the steps to my house with the picture flapping. My mom looks but don't say nothing. She shows my stepdad and says, Look at this shit. What the fuck, my stepdad says. He shoves a black crayon into my hand. His fat hand grabs mine and makes me color over Rhonda's yellow hair. Same to her face with a brown crayon. He says, Now thats better. My mom says, Shonuff is.

Meddling Kids

The cable is off again. Me and my sister turn the knob to all thirteen channels, nothing but static. I aint playing Barbies with you, she says, cuz last time you made He-Man beat up Barbie. Good, I say, I dont wanna play that stupid shit anyway. Well, she says, I'll just pretend to watch teevee. Thats stupid, I say.

My sister sits in front of the teevee. The static is loud. She leans in and says, Zoinks. I sit next to her, What are you watching. None of your beeswax, she says. She starts singing, We got some work to do now. Can I watch too, I say. Okay, she says, but only if you be Shaggy and Scooby, and I'll be the smart ones.

She puts her hands on the steering wheel and says, Gang, we're almost to West Virginia. The mayor called us to investigate a couple of monsters thats been scaring kids all over town. I say, Ruh-roh, Raggy. My sister goes on, Lets split up and look for clues. Velma and Daphne, come with me. Shag and Scoob, start at the cemetery. I chatter my teeth and say, Ruh-roh, not the remetery. My sister says, Gang, we found some clues. We followed a little ugly boy and a pretty girl into a house. We spotted the monsters when they chased the boy and girl out of the house yelling, I'll give you something to cry for. So gang, heres the plan. My sister whispers something in my ear I can't understand. Then she says, Got it, Shaggy and Scoob. Zoinks, I say.

Okay gang, my sister says, we will rescue the kids from the house. But first we gotta sneak in and set up booby traps. My sister stops to think. Okay, she says, I got it now. We will go in and let the monsters see us rescuing the kids. Then they will chase us. Scoob, while theyre chasing us I want you to take this rope and trip them. I say, No way Fred. My sister goes into the kitchen and comes back with a cracker and says, How about a Scooby snack. She throws the cracker in the air and I try to catch it in my mouth but it falls on the floor. I pick it up and eat it. She goes on, After Scoob trips them with the rope, there will be oil and banana peels on the ground and they will slide down a ramp into a dumpster filled with nails and rats and barbwire. And thats when we will take they masks off.

We run through the house saying Zoinks and Yikes. We jump on the couch and dive off. We stick our heads around a corner and run in place. We run in and out of closets. My sister says, Now, Scoob. I put the jump rope in my mouth and dive in front of the door. My sister says, Whooaa – slippy-slip, down the ramp they go. She makes the deep voice of the monsters, Why is these rats bitin my ass – Who put barbwire in this goddamn dumpster. My sister grabs a baseball bat and opens the trash can. She says, These monsters look like our mom and stepdad. C'mon Shaggy, take them goddamn masks off.

Happy Little Trees

Bob Ross is on. He has paint. I don't. First I grind flowers with a rock but it don't work. I chew and chew dandelions. Spit mixes into yellow paste. I chew grass. I chew mulberries. I chew wild onions. They don't make color so I swallow. Tingles back of the neck and waters my eyes.

Chew coal. Chew red clay. Chew what a grasshopper chews. I chew a grasshopper. Crunchy, then juice squirts to back of throat. The paste is chunky brown green white. Lick off hand and chew until smooth. Open jar, chew lightning bugs. Wait till night when they light, then rip off the ass, smear it on my face.

Heavy D

I'm trying to teach my sister a song I recorded off the radio. Listen real close, I say.

One two, she says, tell me something about coins and a jackpot.

Goddammit, I say, you got it wrong – its not that hard.

Shut up, she says, this is stupid. Why do I need to learn this anyway.

Cuz its important like the Pledge of Allegiance.

I know the chorus, she says, Now that we found love what are we gonna doo.

That aint enough, I say. You gotta learn the whole thing.

Why. Since you already know it, you rap and I sing.

No. What if I cant talk one day. And if you dont know it, then who will.

Okay, she says, just go slow next time.

I rap the first two lines. She gets it. I add more. She gets that. After an hour she gets the last lines: I'm not quite sure of what is going down, but I'm feeling hunky-dory bout this thing that I found. I rewind the tape and we rap the song three times perfect.

She says, If you actually found love what would you do with it.

Thats a stupid question.

No it aint, she says. Just answer it. What would you do with love.

Dust

My mom and stepdad have a baby so we move in with my stepdad's mama. The house is built on the side of a hill. The house is leaning. The house has a kitchen floor that is slanted with the tops of nails pushing through brown linoleum. The house has a basement with a coal furnace. The house is white with two bedrooms upstairs, a bedroom and kitchen and living room downstairs. My mom and stepdad and the baby sleep in the living room. LaShawn and Jamar are my stepdad's niece and nephew. They sleep in the bed with my stepdad's mama in the bedroom downstairs. In the same room me and my sister sleep on the floor. Nobody sleeps upstairs.

When I put coal on the fire before bed a rat waddles along the wooden beams and stops to look down at me. Now while I'm trying to sleep I hear the rat scratching and chewing wood under the floor.

At five my stepdad yells to wake me to put coal on the fire. He says I didn't fix it good enough last night at one. He says if I fixed it good enough I could sleep till five thirty. I walk outside and go to the basement. I shovel two buckets of ashes from the bottom of the furnace and dump them over the hill. Then I fill seven buckets of coal and dump three on the fire so it will last until I come from school.

Me and my sister, and LaShawn and Jamar, come from school. My stepdad yells because the fire went out. He said he and his mama and the baby was cold all day. That I was trying to freeze them to death. LaShawn and Jamar ask me why can't I fix the fire right. My mom tells me I better get my shit together. I go to the basement and the fire is out. I put too much coal on and smothered it. I need to build a new fire.

There's an old house next door where I get dry wood. With the axe I chop brittle walls, kick through walls, chop up the floor. Wake the rats. Their nest is tangled straw, sticks and dry leaves. In it is chewed-up Bible pages. Empty can of potted meat. Cracked pork-chop bones. Half-eaten Barbie head.

At five the next morning I put three buckets of coal on the fire so it will last until I come from school.

Shake to Erase

I did something bad, at school or at home, maybe school, probably home.

I'm thinking of how to draw a face on my Etch A Sketch how to draw the eyes and eyebrows without drawing a line across the top of the nose I'd have to draw one eye and make the eyebrow really bushy then from the corner of the eye I'd have to draw the nose down and around and back up and do another eye then I'd have to trace the nose back down to the bottom and make a mustache so the line won't show where it need to connect to make lips but how do I get to the chin and the outside of the face without showing a line.

Start over Shake.

Stepdad hits me again, extension cord, or switch. Oh, you aint cryin. You think you a man, I'll beat you like one.

Start with the hairline then draw a beard like how I'd do the mustache then draw the lips up to the nose and eyes then do the eyebrows last trace the nose back down to the lips and chin and draw a neck then draw a city in the background draw lines up and across and down and make different sizes of skyscrapers then trace over the top of the man's head and draw more buildings on the other side then turn the knob all the way to the edge and go all the way up up and draw an airplane in the corner then turn the knob all the way over over to the other corner and draw a sun. Start over Shake.

I pull up my white long johns. Stripes soak through. Red zebra.

Two Times Two

My uncle, Mom's brother, picks me and my friend Mack up from school early. Mack's dad is driving. He says we gotta go to Pocahontas, Virginia to handle some business. He stops at the filling station. My uncle gives me and Mack some money and tells us to buy a big bag of Funyuns and MoonPies and Salem 100's and a bottle of Wild Irish Rose, the big bottle.

Mack's dad speeds downhill around curves while we slide back and forth across the backseat and raise our hands like on a roller coaster and we say, Whoo, faster faster. He goes faster. We pass around the Funyuns and eat our MoonPies. Mack says, Dangit, Dad, we aint buy no sodas, I'm thirsty. My uncle hands the bottle of Wild Irish Rose to us and says, Dont drink too much, this aint no Kool-Aid.

With both hands Mack tips the bottle to his lips and says, Ahh, it taste like Kool-Aid. He gives me the bottle. It do taste like Kool-Aid, I say. They laugh. I give the bottle to my uncle, he drinks, gives it to Mack's dad, he drinks, gives it to Mack, he drinks, gives it back to me. It goes like this until we get to Pocahontas.

We cross train tracks and park behind a brick building. The roof is caved in and windows half busted out. Poison ivy crawls up the side. My uncle says, You turkeys hold tight, we'll be back in a few ticks. Mack, I say, look at your dad. We make fun of Mack's dad because he has a jerry curl tied in a baby ponytail and wears the same thing every day: a red-and-black track suit and black Chuck Taylors. His pants are high and you can see his white socks. His stomach sticks out and he never wears a shirt under his jacket. He wears a gold rope chain with a bunny on it resting in his curly chest hair. Mack says, So, look at your uncle. My uncle got on blue jean bell-bottoms with a brown leather jacket. A blue-jean floppy hat. He don't have a shirt on under his jacket either. They walk to a house with white paint peeling off. Half of the porch droops. A big Doberman is tied to a tree in the dirt yard. It keeps barking and running until the chain yanks it back.

Mack says, Lets see if we can bust out the rest of the windows. We throw rocks at the top windows. Mack is the first one to hit glass. He says, Thats why I'm the pitcher and you play leftfield. So, I say, I betcha I'll hit way more than you. We throw more. He keeps hitting glass. I don't. Mack says, I wanna practice my fastball. I find a broken broomstick next to the brick building. Mack collects a shirt-full of coal and rocks from the train tracks.

Mack throws a piece of coal. I swing, but it feels real slow. I'm getting a little woobly. See, Mack says, I told you my fastball was fast. Mack raises his leg to pitch but he woobles a bit. He laughs, I dont know whats wrong with me. He throws a piece of coal high in the air. I swing. Hit. It explodes. Dust powders my face. Mack laughs. Me too. Mack throws another. I miss. Mack says, You like Rhonda dontcha.

Hell no, I say, who told you that. I seen that picture with yall holding hands, he says. I aint draw no picture of nobody, I say.

Whats taking them so long, I say. I dont know, Mack says, but I'm getting thirsty again. I think they left that bottle in the car, I say. We get the bottle and sit on the steps of the brick building. I drink, give it to Mack, he drinks, gives it back. It goes like this until it starts to get dark. You ever smoke before, Mack says. I took a puff of my uncles Salem one time, I say. I smoke all the time, he says. We search the car for the Salems but don't find none. We can smoke leaves, Mack says, my cousin do it all the time. Mack tears a piece of paper out of his notebook. He picks some poison ivy off of the building. He rolls it into the paper and licks the seam. Thats nasty, I say, I dont wanna smoke your spit. I have to do that, he says, so it will stick. Mack lights the paper. He sucks on it. Coughs a little cough. Smoke rolls out his nose and mouth. He gives it me. I do the same but don't cough. Mack says, You didnt inhale. You gotta make the smoke go in your lungs. I try again. Take a deep breath, Mack says. I choke. Smoke shoots out my mouth and nose. I drool on my shirt. Eyes water. I look at Mack. His face is melting. Mack smokes, gives it to me, I smoke, give it back. It goes like this until Mack's dad and my uncle stumble out with their arms around each other. Their slow brown faces laughing and smoking.

In the car Mack's dad says, What happened to all the Rose. My uncle laughs and says, Them turkeys drunk it all. Oh well, Mack's dad says. My uncle says, Shit, we forgot to tell yall turkeys do ya homework. What yall got anyway. Um, I say, we sposed to be learning our times tables. Oh yeah, Mack says, we gotta do these worksheets. I hate times tables, I say, its too hard. My uncle says, Aw hell, it aint that damn hard. He takes out a pack of Salems and says, Look, its twenty cigarettes in this one pack. If you had two packs how many would that be. Forty, I say. Good, he says, you just did twenty times two. Now if you had three packs, how many is that. Mack says, Sixty. Good, my uncle says, thats twenty times three. Now do the same with all the times tables, just keep adding. See, that shit is easy aint it. Mack's dad turns the yellow light on in the top of the car so we can do the worksheets. All the way home my uncle makes us recite all the twos to the twelves over and over.

Mack's dad drives up on the hill to drop me and Uncle off. Everybody is in the street with the sheriff. My mom runs up and slaps my uncle in the face, Where the hell yall been, she says, I thought his dad kidnapped him, why you aint tell nobody you picked him up, you drunk muthafucka. My uncle says, Be cool, Jack. That boy is fine. My mom slaps him again. My uncle says, I said chill the fuck out. He did his homework and we fed him. My mom says, I had enough of you, you fuckin drunkard, got my kid runnin the streets, had me thinkin his dad kidnapped him. My uncle grabs my shoulders and kisses me on the forehead. He hugs me and says, Alright Turkey, get some rest and have a good day at school tomorrow. My lungs and my throat feel weird. My mom grabs me and says, Look at me boy, whats wrong with you. I throw up on her feet.

Bunt

My stepdad has a long white Chrysler with cushy green seats. He picks all the kids up on our baseball team from all their houses. We pile onto each other's laps. Music is blasting and laughing while he swings the car around curves. He starts practice by hitting balls to us in the infield, then outfield. The ting of the ball on the aluminum bat sounds like the slap on my forearm for mosquitoes. Then we run laps, giving him a high five each time we round home plate. On the way home he buys each of us a bag of chips. He does the same thing the next day and the next day. He does the same thing during football season.

Dance

Jamar and my sister are in the same class. We come from school and Jamar tells everybody that my sister stood on her desk and took her clothes off and sang, Do the Humpty-Hump. She was just like this, he says and stands in the chair and twists his hips and rubs his stomach while pulling up his shirt. My mom says to my sister, You a whore, huh, showin ya ass in public. Jamar keeps dancing on the chair and saying, Yep, she was just like this.

Some words are boiling in my belly and pushing up through my chest, my chest tries to trap these words, but these words keep pushing up like puke, and my mouth spews, Stop fuckin lying Jamar.

Watch ya fuckin mouth, my mom says, who told you talk when aint nobody talkin to ya little dumb ass. Stupid muthafucka, my stepdad says, you the fuckin liar. You gonna get it now, my mom says. LaShawn and Jamar laugh. My stepdad says, I know thats right, you betta whoop his ass before he try to whoop yours.

My mom tells me to pull my pants down and bend over the stool. She is having a hard time choosing between the belt and the extension cord. Until my stepdad says, Use this, and gives her a big stick. I'm thinking of how to draw a face on my Etch A Sketch.

We

Last night I dreamed that me and my sister were in front of the house playing hopscotch. After I won, cuz I always win, we sat on the porch. We were laughing. Somebody drives up and shoots my sister in the chest.

I wake up the next day and while we walk down the hill to the bus stop I keep looking at my sister to see if she is okay. She looks at me and says, You okay. Yeah, I say, why. Cuz, she says, last night I had a dream that me and you was in front of our house playing hopscotch. And after I won, cuz I always win, we was sitting on the porch laughing. And somebody drove up and shot you in the chest.

Yellow

Everyone is downstairs crying. I walk upstairs to Grandma's room. It is dark. Her dirty pink house shoes are lined up by the nightstand like she just got into bed. The covers on her side are pulled back like she just got out of bed. I leave and ask my mom how Grandma died. My mom says she just turned yellow and died. What, I say. You heard me, she says, she just turned yellow and died. I will never eat dandelions again.

Playground

We have a new girl that just moved from Africa. Gambia. I looked it up in my atlas and it looks like a crooked little finger in the middle of Senegal. Her name is Anter Jatta. I say it over and over. Anter Jatta. She is really dark and pretty. Everybody else says she is black and ugly. Buck says she is so black if she wore yellow lipstick she would look like a cheeseburger. He says this in front of her because she don't understand English that much. She smiles. Her teeth are really white and straight.

I make sure I wear my African sign every day. I even wear my Afro pick with the fist on the end. At recess by the monkey bars I say to her, My beautiful Sister, what is it like in the Mother Land. The man tries to hold us down in America. I know about Senegal too. She smiles.

I walk back to the basketball court and Buck says, I see you over there tryin to hook up with that African booty scratcher. No way, I say, I was just telling her how black she was. Its okay to hook up with her, he says. Buck knows a lot because this is his third time in sixth grade. He explains, She probably got some wet jungle pussy, its neon pink. Can you imagine how wet that pussy hair is. You can swing from it like vines. All African girls cut they pussy hair in the shape of a African sign, they even dye it red, yellow, and green.

When recess is over, me and Buck walk by Anter Jatta. I raise my fist and say, Solid. Buck says, Whats up, jungle pussy. She smiles.

Who Knows

We have one homeless man in our town. Everybody calls him the Man in Black. Because that's all he wears is black, most of the black is coal dust, plus he is dark skinned. He is really tall and his dirty hands look like bear paws and his big boots thud the ground with each stride. He lives in a saggy brown canvas tent next to the creek at the bottom of the mountain. In the winter you can see the blue flame from his kerosene heater glowing inside the tent. He never talks to nobody.

I see him in the store sometimes buying bread and baloney with a hundred-dollar bill. Thats because he gets a crazy check, they say. Some people say he went crazy in the war. Some say he just went crazy. Some say he sold his soul to Satan. My uncle says he is a righteous revolutionary brother who spits in the man's face. My grandma says he used to be married to a white woman and she took everything he had and now he don't want shit to do with nothing white, especially no stankin-ass white folks.

When I'm behind the Man in Black in the store he stinks so bad my stomach hurts. He turns around, looks down at me, sees me frowning and covering my nose, and says, I dont smell no worse than ya drunk-ass uncle.

Trouble

My aunt, Mom's sister, says me and my sister are in trouble and we need to come down to her house asap. I already know why. And I told my dumb-ass sister not to call the Care Bear Hotline. Imma whoop yalls ass good when you get back, my mom says, You ran up her phone bill a hundred dollars. My aunt says, Dont worry, Imma take care of it.

While we walk to our aunt's house I keep telling my sister she is stupid and I'm gonna say I aint have shit to do with it. She knows our stepdad don't like us going down there, and you done fucked it up, I say. Shut up, she says, you was there so its your fault too.

We walk in our aunt's house and she is sitting on the couch with the phone bill on top of a book in her lap. She takes off her glasses, Why'd you do it. My sister says, I dont know, I'm sorry. I know youre sorry, she says, but you know why you called the Care Bears. Um, my sister says, I guess I just wanted to talk. Well, my aunt says, dont worry, this is a diminutive problem we can take care of. Diminutive is my aunt's favorite word. She says it a lot. Especially when she talks about her shot glasses she collects when she travels. Cmon in the kitchen, she says. We walk through the hall past her long bookshelf. Oh, she says, I have a glass from San Francisco to add to my diminutive glass collection.

My aunt starts frying fish and telling me and my sister about a new book she is reading. A moving mystery, she says, but with literary sensibilities. I'm trying to write a book too, I say, its kind of a mystery, cuz I don't know whats going to happen, its diminutive so far cuz I just started, but I want it to be not diminutive when I finish. Well hell, she says, you gotta show me this book.

We all sit at the kitchen table eating fried fish, hot sauce and little bones and grease everywhere. My aunt leaves and comes back with the telephone. Here, she says to my sister, you can call them again if you want. ∎

Interior: Monkeyboy, 2013
Courtesy of the artist

INTERIOR: MONKEYBOY

Patrick Flanery

I find him in front of the painting. Though you can't tell much about the boy in the picture, he must be about the same age as the boy standing there on the carpet in the living room, the boy who is now, I remind myself, my son.

'What is it?' the real boy, my son, asks me.

'A painting.'

'What's a painting?'

'A work of art.'

'What's a work of art?'

'Something made by an artist.'

He stares at the painting. I cannot bring myself to say his name, the name that I did not choose, and so instead I call him by the name I would give him if he were mine to name, that is to say, I call him Will in my mind and almost nothing to his face except *you*, or worse still, I address him indirectly, making statements that fail to acknowledge him as the implied subject.

Will looks from the painting to me, his eyes bugging out.

'Someone *made that*?'

'Yes, the artist made it.'

'But how did he make it?'

'She.'

'What?'

'The artist is a woman,' I say.

'Oh.' As his eyes flick back to the painting he puts his index finger in his ear, like sliding a key into a lock, then takes it out again. 'What's her name?'

'Kate.'

Will turns from the boy in the painting to glance around the room in the flat he has been getting to know over the course of the past couple of days, before looking back at the painting once more. 'How did she make it?'

'With oil paint and a brush and a canvas and varnish and turpentine, I suppose.'

'What's turpatine?'

'Turpentine's a chemical. Made from pine trees.'

'The painting is made from *trees*?'

'In a way, yes. Part of it is. And there's a stretcher behind the canvas, and the stretcher is made of wood.'

'And the cavas?'

'The *can*vas. It's made of cotton.'

'Like a shirt?'

'Yes, like a shirt, but both the shirt and the canvas come from a plant.'

'Oh.'

'Have you ever made a piece of art?'

Will glares at me as if I'm stupid, his features drooping in an arrangement he must have learned from a teacher, perhaps older children, or even the man and woman who called themselves his parents before Edward and I began calling ourselves his parents a few days ago. 'Not like *that*.'

'At school? Have you never painted?'

He makes a show of thinking, cocks his head.

'Once or twice, I guess.'

'We'll get out the materials this weekend. You can try your hand at making art. I bet you'll like painting.'

'I *like* dancing,' he says, still studying the image of the boy standing in a living room, the painted child's head three-quarters turned towards the viewer, as if gazing not at his real-world observers but at someone else in the house where he stands, someone just outside the frame of the painting. It is difficult to tell what the boy in the painting feels, what his mood might be, although the hands on his slim hips suggest determination, even willfulness.

Later, after dinner, I find Will standing in the same place, staring at the painting, then at our living room, as though trying to make sense of some implied relation between the image on the wall and the space surrounding the image. At dinner he refused to eat mushrooms and threw one across the kitchen, leaving a gray-brown streak of roasted portobello trickling down the wall. He threw his fork and knife across the tiled floor and pushed himself back in the chair, kicking the legs of the table, his arms crossed over his chest. Textbook tantrum. We have had training, my husband and I, we know how to respond to such provocations. Instead of time-outs, as with a 'normal' child, Will earns 'time-ins': time spent with us attending to him in a way that feels like a performance of parenting rather than parenting itself. It is still easier than in the excruciating workshops in which we took turns playing a child with an attachment disorder and the parent who would work to strengthen those tenuous bonds.

Edward and I put him to bed in the room we prepared over the past six months with no sense of who might one day sleep inside it, boy or girl, younger or older. Will is older than we first wanted, but the introductory meetings went well, and the file revealed nothing but neglect and deprivation, as if neglect and deprivation were minor considerations. In fact they were, compared to the scores of children whose mothers drank and drugged their way through pregnancy, or children physically and sexually abused, born months prematurely, or who happened to be unlucky inheritors of a chromosomal disorder or some other disease, carrying with them a large degree of uncertainty about their long-term development, or kids who suffered from global developmental delay, insecure attachment disorders, and so forth.

Enough to make any sane person despair, and yet we had chosen to take this route rather than any other. Altruism, Edward said, it's about altruism. Or naked self-sacrifice, I countered. This had not been my original impulse, not what I imagined when I first thought about how, in the absence of biological ability, we might have a child, but in Britain, unlike America, there are scarcely any babies available to adopt from birth. If only I had forced Edward to move to my country rather than staying in his, where there are comparatively so few children available to adopt, and where surrogacy is all but impossible.

On paper, Will is 'normal', just neglected. He looks reasonably like us, or at least like Edward, and perhaps like me, too, if you were to glimpse us passing through shadow across the street, in the distance, our heads turned three-quarters to face the horizon.

We made a room for him that is ungendered, appropriate for no particular age of child, pale gray walls that are soothing in this city's watery light, a bright red rug on the parquet floor, a white-framed single bed bought at the last minute – last Saturday in fact, when we were certain we needed something larger than a crib.

'Do you like your room?' I asked Will when he arrived. That was Tuesday.

'It's bigger than my last one.' He sat down on the white bedspread, ran the palms of his hands against the cotton, almost, I thought, like a poor person experiencing luxury for the first time. High thread count, Egyptian. As if that were important for a child, for the waif who is in the process of becoming my son. He was afraid of getting it dirty, he told me, and I said he shouldn't worry about that. Things get dirty. But I knew we had made a mistake, created a room too adult for a boy like him. It was a space for the ideal boy, for the boy we might have had if we had been able to produce him ourselves or adopt him from birth, lullabying him beneath a miniature reproduction of an Alexander Calder mobile. For Will there would need to be different bedding, sheets with superheroes or cartoon characters, bedspreads crisscrossed by cars or motorcycles, assuming he was that kind of boy.

'We can change it if you don't like it.'

'You mean for a diff-er-ent room?' He spoke those syllables with halting correctness, as if the word had been hammered into his teeth and tongue. Such crooked teeth. We would be paying for substantial dental work in another few years.

'No, this will still be your room. But we can paint it another color, or change the rug. And maybe you want to put up some pictures.'

'Pictures?'

'Posters, photographs. We can look for things to decorate it. It can be a hunt.'

'A treasure hunt?'

'Yes, a treasure hunt.'

Edward closes our bedroom door. We are getting used to sleeping with the door shut after years of thinking about privacy only when guests came to stay. The first night I found myself locking it and Edward shook his head, as if to say, without saying it, that we can't let him think we don't trust him. He's only a child after all. Yes, but a child we don't know, I wanted to say, tried to say with my eyes and a lift of the shoulders, a hunching forward with my arms, the slight exasperated turn of my hands to face palms to the ceiling, a child with experiences about which we may never know anything for certain, who might get it into his messed-up little head that the two men who now insist on being regarded as his parents are really no better than devils that ought to be slaughtered in their sleep. Edward rolled his eyes, as if to say, again without saying it, too many horror films, too much paranoia, this is not *The Omen*, or whatever film it is that features the psychopathic boy who kills his mother. This is just a child who needs love. We must trust him.

'Do you think he's sleeping well?' Edward asks. 'He seems tired.'

'Some children have trouble sleeping in a new bed. I read it in one of those pamphlets.'

'Might be cumulative fatigue. We don't know what it's been like for him before now.'

'The foster parents seemed all right.'

'I thought they were creepy. They called him the LO. What does that even mean?'

'The Little One.'

Edward groans and rolls his eyes. 'How dreadful.'

'They all use that expression. I didn't think she was so bad. She told me that Will –' I stop myself. It's the first time I've used my name for the boy out loud. Edward's eyebrows lace together. No, not lace – spasm, flinch. I'm confusing my husband, upsetting him. 'I mean . . . Romeo. I don't know what I was thinking. The foster mother, she told me we should watch him. Like a pair of hawks.'

'You see, creepy. She was just trying to scare you,' he says, getting into bed and drawing close to me, breathing into my ear. I feel him harden against my leg.

When I sleep, I dream of Will standing on our bed, flicking a whip against our faces. He draws blood.

This morning Will is up before us, and there he is again, standing in front of the painting I brought back from my last buying trip to Cape Town, discovered in a gallery in the Winelands. Contemporary artist, South African, she paints from found photographs. This piece, like many of her recent works, is slightly blurred, the contours of the living room in which the child stands suggested rather than clearly delineated. Looking at the painting, I feel as if I have fallen into a stranger's memory, with no sense of the outcome or the parameters of its lost narrative. Was the boy in the original photograph wearing a monkey costume, or did the artist add the tail? Why should *this* painting hold my new child's gaze? It is not the only piece of art in the house. There are other paintings and etchings, lithographs and woodcuts, but it's this canvas, of a boy in a living room, a mid-century modern interior, a palette of reds and browns and grays with a prominent slash of white – a vase on the coffee table in the foreground of the painting – that draws him.

'Have you washed already?'

He shakes his head, gives me that 'are you stupid?' glare, and with his hands indicates his clothes, day clothes, going-to-school clothes, a new uniform we bought for his new school. Only his feet are bare. He rises on his tiptoes and kicks his right leg out to the side. Dance or karate?

'Have you had breakfast?'

Twitching his head, he turns back to the painting.

'Come, I'll eat with you. Edward – I mean Dad –'

'Papa.'

'Papa?'

'I'm calling him *Papa*.'

I note to myself: he has called me nothing, not even my name, since arriving on Tuesday. 'Okay. Papa will take you to school this morning. I have a meeting.'

'But I want *you* to take me to school.'

'I can't, Wi—' Terrible. I catch myself. 'I have a meeting today, on the other side of town. I wouldn't make it in time.' It is meant to be the last meeting of the life I am curtailing as of three days ago, the last time I will consult with one of my company's clients, the last time for nearly half a year when I will engage the professional portion of my mind. What, I wonder at night, if the professional is all that is left, and there is no personal share remaining, no individual behind the career? I am the one taking adoption leave, not Edward. I am the one who will be the 'primary carer', as the social worker put it in her horribly nasal drone, which was an improvement over her ungrammatical emails. This meeting is the last commitment from my old life, at least for the next four months. 'How will you make time for a little one in your busy lives?' she asked us during the approval process. 'As any other parents would,' I said, 'we will adapt.'

'You should make the time,' Will says. The adult inflection is as disconcerting as his readiness for school. No doubt it's something he has heard from one of his foster parents, or even his birth parents, father chastising mother or vice versa, the parent who failed to be as available as he or she should have been getting told off by the one who has no choice but to do it all. I know, in fact, I should not frame it with such doubt: neither mother nor father made the time, they both ignored him, did not even feed or clothe him properly, though there was always money for beer, or so Will's file told us.

'It's not nice to speak like that,' I say, trying to flatten my voice.

Then, in a single fluid movement, he reaches out, picks the white ceramic vase from the coffee table and drops it on the floor. I watch it shatter on the parquet, a genuine Stig Lindberg reptile vase that I took months to source after buying the painting, part of the process of making the room match the art. I scream, a reflex, but Will – Romeo – smiles. 'You should *make* the time,' he says quietly, and puts his hands on his hips, scrutinizing the room, as if searching for something else to destroy. I see the mid-century couches ruined, the sliver of coffee table smashed, the television in its reproduction retro housing kicked in by a six-year-old foot.

'I can't. And because of what you've just done, you lose all your screen time for a week.' The punishment is unduly harsh, but it's too late to reverse course. A day's worth of no screen time would have been adequate: a week for a boy his age is eternity.

He grunts and stomps his foot, bare sole coming down hard on an edge of broken pottery, and then he is the one screaming without thought, tears erupting from his eyes, snot from the nose, boy become fountain. I lift him up in my arms, he puts his hands around my neck, sobbing, and I carry him to the bathroom. Edward pushes open the door, his face red, as if he has already decided that I must be to blame, or so I imagine.

'What the hell happened?'

'Why are you *yelling*?' Will wails.

I explain to my husband, I wash the cut in the boy's foot, I see that it's too serious simply to be bandaged, the bleeding is slow to stop, the tub is pink and crimson and white. In a different context it would be beautiful.

'We'll have to go to the hospital.'

'I'll take him,' Edward offers, as if he thinks I might not be up to the task.

'No, really, it's okay.'

'Your meeting.'

'I can reschedule.'

A t the hospital there is a security alert. A car has been abandoned outside the emergency entrance and a dozen police cars are surrounding it, blocking traffic, lights flashing, cones and police tape cordoning off half the street. I watch as an officer breaks the driver's side window and reaches into the car. I hold my breath, expecting the vehicle to explode, but nothing happens. The fifteen-foot-tall Victorian wrought-iron gate to the car park has been chained shut and we have to find a spot several streets away.

'I can't walk,' Will says, as I help him out of the passenger seat. 'It hurts too much.'

'I'll carry you,' I say, imagining what the hospital staff and social workers will think, the questions they will inevitably ask. I wonder if I can carry him the whole distance, but the neglect that Will suffered means he is smaller and lighter than a six-year-old should be. He climbs me, clings to my neck, holds on, surveilling the road behind us. I inhale his odor: white bread soaked in sweet milk, a dusting of cinnamon, a faint note of coffee and cardamom, and then his head is nuzzling my hair and a balloon of warmth expands in my chest.

'I'm too heavy.'

'No, you are very light.'

'Like air?' he says into my ear, almost whispering.

'Even lighter.'

B y the time we get home from the hospital it is after noon. Blessedly few questions from the staff, and instead an understanding from the nurses and the attending doctor that these accidents happen, a gash on the foot is not the kind of thing an abusive parent might inflict, although come often enough with strange wounds and they would have to wonder: abusive, sadistic, or ill. My mother once had a patient with Munchausen's by proxy. Though confident of my innocence, I feel the guilt of speculation.

'What about school?' Will asks.

'No school today.'

'But I'll get in trouble.'

'You won't. I'll phone them. You need to heal. Keep your weight off the foot. We'll have a long weekend instead.'

'What will we do?'

This is the moment I have been dreading since we started the process more than two years ago. With an infant it would have been easy, no expectation of entertainment at first, just routine care, the instincts of parenting, months and years to get used to each other before demands for entertainment would ever be articulated. What does one do to occupy a child of six all day? Can a boy that age not amuse himself? No, unwise: a boy like Will might fill the hours by emptying my home of all that I cherish. Art, objects, mementoes of travel accumulated over the course of my life. I am not prepared to sacrifice such things for the sake of a child's entertainment.

I look at the painting across the living room, the image of the boy gazing at the person absent from the picture, the white vase on the impression of a coffee table, the painting in the background of the painting, the wall lamps, the specter of couches and cushions, the old-fashioned television, a world that is recognizable, a mirror of the room I have created around it, but as if seen through a scrim that both separates and distorts. Art, I think. Art is a thing I know how to do. I am, after all, a professional.

'We could do some painting.'

'Painting my bedroom?'

'Painting a picture.'

'Like making art?'

'Yes, making art.'

Will nods.

Where will it be safe? A mushroom stain easily washed off the kitchen wall, and we can begin with watercolors, nothing too permanent, something that will wipe clean from tiles and granite. We used washable paint in the kitchen, the floor repels everything that falls on it, the cabinets are metal and glass. Watercolor, even if splattered, cannot do much harm in a kitchen. From the materials cupboard in my study I get out tubes of paint, brushes and two large spiral-bound pads of watercolor paper. Will limps behind me as I lay a drop cloth on the counter and drape old towels over two of the kitchen stools. The floor can look after itself. I open the pads of paper next to each other on the counter, squirt paint onto the two palettes, and fill empty tuna cans with water from the tap. I tell Will to change into old clothes, and then realize he has no old clothes, he has hardly any clothes to his name, coming to us with a single duffel bag of belongings: seven pairs of underwear, seven pairs of socks, two sets of his old school uniform, a couple pairs of jeans, shorts, shirts and T-shirts, one coat, no hat or scarf, two pairs of shoes, no toys or books or other possessions.

'A white T-shirt,' I say, 'or that black one you have, and a pair of shorts.'

'I only have school shorts.'

'What about the ones from your old uniform?'

He hesitates.

'You won't need them again. Different colors at your new school.' Is it wrong to feel pleasure at being able to provide with such confidence, to assure the child in my care that what he has struggled to maintain may now be discarded with impunity? There will always be more, cheap, until it all runs out, or the world upends itself.

When he has changed, I help him onto the stool and show him how to dip the brush first in the water, then in the paint, and begin to apply color to the paper, deciding to let him experiment, not to be too prescriptive. Let him make mistakes, allow him to see what happens with too much water, the way the paper will begin to curl and undulate.

'What should I paint?' he asks me.

'Whatever you like.'

'But I don't know what to paint.' He rolls his eyes, pouting a little.

'Paint yourself. Do a self-portrait.'

'A picture of my*self*?'

Why should this seem so preposterous to him? Because no one has ever suggested to him that he is worth representing?

'Why not?'

He pushes his face to a point, brows and lips forced outward as though trying to join up with the tip of his nose. 'Okay, maybe I could do that,' he says, and chooses a brush, dips the brush first in the water and then in the orange paint, which he applies to the paper in a circle. He fills in the circle and on either side of it paints two arcs, and then at the base of the circle a long post, out of which protrude four smaller posts: a stick-figure self, naked. I try to occupy myself with my own painting, to let him work without feeling observed. A memory of a Paul Klee exhibition leads my own hand to an irregular grid of colors, a flattened Harlequin, or a clown crushed by a steamroller. Will dips his brush in the water, swirls it about, and then jabs it into a worm of blue paint. Wet on wet. He will either be captivated by the possibility of colors blurring, or distressed by the imprecision of the result. As the blue enters the orange, they combine into a greenish-brown arc where he has intended to paint a shirt. He quickly withdraws the brush and watches as the color spreads.

'It's messy.'

'Wet colors run, but it's fine, there's nothing wrong with that.'

'Your one isn't messy,' he says.

'No, but I use less water, and there are different kinds of paintings.' I show him some reproductions of work by Marlene Dumas, wet on wet. 'You can make any kind of painting you want. Just experiment.'

'Espeeramet?'

How his accent grates. It will have to be ironed, flattened, dried out.

'Try things. See what happens. Don't worry what it's going to look like in the end. Just get a feel for the medium, the paints.' I catch myself being prescriptive even in my desire to liberate.

He tries again, brush against the paper, blue into orange, feathery blurs of color. This is a child who wants precision, who has undoubtedly been required to stay within the lines of coloring books, whose teachers have praised tidiness rather than creativity. His parents – the first people who called themselves his parents, who forfeited the right to call this boy their son – probably shouted at him if he made a mess. I can imagine the foster parents, a couple in their sixties, rough in their speech but tidy in their habits, house-proud with net curtains and silk flowers, shouting at Will if he stepped out of line. His clothes arrived clean, pressed, folded in that duffel bag, the spare shoes wrapped in plastic, all of it, every stitch, manufactured in China, perhaps even by children like Will. When I think of China I think of regimentation, the management of nature, everything controlled and precise, chaos pushed to the edges or hidden behind façades. This, I note, is the Year of the Fire Monkey, a year of change.

Will throws his brush down on the counter and grunts through his nose in frustration. Watercolor was the wrong choice. Crayons, colored pencils, fine-tipped Magic Markers, those would have been better.

Will is in bed after calling George and Henry names so rude even they, usually unflappable, are shocked. Where could he have learned that language, except from adults? Surely no child his age would know such artful obscenities. For half an hour after being put to bed, he continued to scream. I worry what the neighbors will think, and then, as if my psychological evolution is outpacing my expectations, I find that I no longer care about neighbors.

'I'm sorry, guys,' I say, 'I hoped he might behave for company. One of my many recent miscalculations.'

'He's very alpha for a six-year-old,' George says, pouring himself a second vodka.

'I fear what may be coming in a few years' time, sweetie,' says Henry. 'Are you ready for all the teenage issues?'

'He's only six.'

'Ten is the new fifteen,' George says, 'I have godsons, my dear, I *know*.'

I glance at Edward, giving him the tight smile that says this is exactly what I predicted would happen and he should have trusted me in the first place.

'It's going to be fine. He's had a difficult start,' Edward says, and I find his confidence as maddening as it is reassuring. I want to say: You have not spent the day with him, you cannot imagine the difficulty of scrubbing blue and orange handprints off the living-room walls as the child who is now your son threatens to throw himself from the balcony to his death because he hates you. 'We will all adjust, and things will calm down. Love conquers all.'

'Love does not conquer trauma. Only psychoanalysis can help you there,' George says.

'Or pharmaceuticals,' says Henry, smirking. 'I know a doctor who will give you *anything* if you switch on the tears.'

'If he wasn't happy painting, what *does* the boy like to do?' George asks.

'He says he likes to dance.'

'But *you* like to dance, darling. You used to be so good at it.'

'You should teach him to tango,' Henry laughs. 'That's a dance which is all about governing rage.'

He wakes me up, pushing a space between Edward and me, and then, after a minute, begins to breathe a stately waltz of sleep. It is too dark for me to see Edward's face, but I hear his head turn, his mouth open, and I know that if we could look into each other's eyes, we would both be smiling, brows crinkled in expressions of empathy, or sympathy, for the troubled child at rest. Will's arm twitches, not pushing my husband and me apart, I try to tell myself, but pushing out a space for himself, opening a compartment within the us that already is, expanding our sense of the we as we've known it.

Saturdays are always hopeful. Will comes tiptoeing into the kitchen, rubbing his eyes, a flag of hair flying after being pressed into place by ten hours in bed. I wash the wound on his sole, examine the stitches, and he winces when I wrap it again and pull on the sock. This is your own doing, I want to say, but know that is both true and not. His doing was the work of other hands, those of the absent birth parents who created this beast – no, child – who breaks what is precious to someone else and, when chastised, injures himself in retort: a piece of brutalist performance art. Someone should give those birth parents the Turner Prize. We could open our home as a gallery space, stage nightly performances for a limited run. I might turn myself from a designer back into an artist, take the credit, sign my name to the work of my child.

After I have cleaned up the cotton swabs and tissues from dressing Will's wound, I give him a bowl of cereal. He picks flakes from the milk and arranges them in a smiley face on the kitchen table, checking out of the corner of his eye to see if I will scold him. Edward does the work for me.

'Don't play with your food, my boy,' he says, smoothing Will's riot of hair back into place. I wait for our child to react, and Will seems to be waiting to see how he himself will respond. He looks from Edward to me and back to Edward, then picks each flake of cereal from the counter and puts it in his mouth before finishing all the food in his bowl. This is the child corrected, trying to be good, and yet I struggle to smile, to reward him for doing as he has been told. We need to have a conversation about words, the words he used last night. The later we leave it, the harder it will become, but Edward has to attend a symposium, and either I will do it alone, or it will have to wait until this evening, and that, I feel certain, will be too late to have the proper effect, to make Will see that calling our friends names is unacceptable, that there are limits to our capacity to accept his behavior, that he must mold himself into a different version of the boy he has been up to this point in time. I would rather do it with Edward, but it must happen now, so I wait until my husband is out the door and then sit down across the kitchen table from Will. He turns his spoon upside down and a trickle of milk dribbles along the steel edge.

'You seemed very angry last night,' I say, holding out my hand to him. He looks at my palm as if he does not know what to do with it, then puts his own hands in his lap, leaving mine there, naked, abandoned.

'No.'

'Those were angry words you used with our friends.'

His features pull together again into a point, his head twitches, he makes animal noises, clicks his tongue against his palate and scratches his armpit. Is this acknowledgment or refusal? I need less ambiguous sign language.

'Do you know what those words mean?'

He shakes his head. Quite clear this time.

'Where did you hear them?'

'Can we dance?' he asks.

'No, not right now. We're talking about words.'

'But I want to dance.'

He gets up and shuffles across the kitchen to the stereo, switches it on, prods the tuner button until he finds a station he likes, turns up the volume, and begins throwing his arms in the air. A chimpanzee, I think, an orangutan. The song is not one I have heard, on a station I would never choose, but Will knows the words and sings along with the girl on the radio, lyrics about moving furniture to dance. When his back is turned, I slip past him, turn off the radio, and stand with my arms folded across my chest. He spins around and growls at me, then hurtles forward, palms out, and pushes me backwards against the counter, throwing me off balance so I hit my head on the cabinet. Half the room goes black and the other half ripples with small silver explosions. I stagger, put my hand to the back of my head, feel moisture and stickiness.

'Sit down!' I scream. 'Sit down right now!'

Will cowers, huddling in the corner near the door to the living room. He pulls out the cutlery drawer and crouches beneath it, arms wrapped around his shaking legs.

The same nurse is on duty as last time.

'It's you today, I see,' he says, ripping open the cover on a sterile swab.

'My son pushed me. Yesterday he broke my favorite vase and cut himself on it, today he pushes me into a cabinet.'

The nurse gives me a look, as if he thinks I might deserve it, then shakes his head. 'I see it more than you'd think,' he says, and leaves me holding a compress as I wait for the doctor. X-rays, no concussion, stitches, a bandage. A minor incident in family life, I suppose, for the vast majority of people with children. To me it seems like a crisis from which we may not recover. I imagine returning Will to the department store where we bought his bed, asking for another model, one that is not quite so defective, but Edward and I agreed, no matter what, we would not give up on this boy. 'Altruism,' I said to Edward when we made the decision, 'weighs significantly more than love.'

'How do you mean?' he asked.

'I feel it on my shoulders already,' I said, and he took me in his arms, plumping me upright.

When I come out to reception, Edward and Will are sitting hunched over a coloring book, an adult coloring book, one of those intricately designed things composed of botanical and animal motifs, each leaf a maze of competing patterns, every feather a mosaic of byzantine complexity. Will is focused on a frog, working hard to stay in the lines of the serpentine forms that make up its legs.

'What do you say, Romeo?' Edward prompts the boy who, if we all play nicely and adjust to one another, will legally be our son in a matter of eight weeks, from which point onward dissolution will become much more difficult, might require, for all I know, me declaring myself an unfit parent.

'Sorry,' the boy mumbles.

'Sorry for what?'

'Sorry for pushing you,' says the boy.

'How about a kiss?' says Edward.

No, I want to say, I do not want a kiss from that little beast, but

I lean over and let him embrace me, his arms circling my neck, hot breath landing with a smack alongside my nose.

At dinner, I allow my husband and this boy who breaks my belongings and attacks me without provocation to do all the talking. How have they bonded so easily? I do not laugh at the boy's jokes. I refuse him eye contact. I clear the dishes, I ask Edward to see to the boy's bath and bedtime. I have a headache, I say. I take a painkiller and grip the edge of the sink, looking out on the communal gardens of the development, listening to the buses pass, the sirens running to the hospital, and, down the hall, the sound of laughter, the boy and my husband joking, joshing, getting on so well with each other. This was not what I signed up for. I will phone the social worker on Monday morning and tell her to come get the boy. The bed can still be returned to the department store – the frame at least. I'll donate the mattress. Health and safety rules. Contamination. Does no one think how a feral child might contaminate its nest? We will start over, remortgage the flat, hire a California surrogate. I do not want to spend the rest of my life fixing someone else's failure.

'You can't continue to punish him,' Edward says, after we have gone to bed.

'He needs to know he can't behave like that.'

'I think he knows. He's just a boy.'

'He's not a boy. He's an animal. We can't keep him. He has to go back,' I say, as Edward suddenly seizes my hand, staring past me. I turn my head, and Will is there in his pajamas, standing in the light of the doorway, his face scrambled and wet, features drawn to that terrible point. Pinched, I think, I have acquired an English child with pinched features. How much I would rather have one of my own, an American baby with no early trauma other than separation from its biological parents, a child I could hold from the moment of birth. Looking at the tears on the face of the boy I agreed to turn into my son, I wait for the ballooning of love in my chest, but nothing comes, no breath of affection.

The boy turns and runs down the hall, Edward springing from our bed to go after him. I listen to the crying and beneath it the murmur of Edward's consolations. He is good at consolation, as he is good at almost everything, perhaps save self-interest or introspection, or the development of an inner life. I wonder sometimes if my husband is ever contemplative, or is instead as purely animal as he so often seems – animal in the best sense, of course, natural and responsive and fit, a thing of nature within nature. Consolation is an animal trait. Pet videos have proved it to us. The behavior of elephants, too, in a time of death. What is their mourning if not an act of group consolation?

At the start of this process, we agreed that Edward would be the parent who said no, because he has an instinct for comfort, for making rejection palatable. I am too likely to snap and bark (too human, I think, or too like an animal that has been mistreated and so becomes unnatural), and as a consequence I must be the one who always says yes, even if that yes is qualified by the admonition, 'but ask Papa what he thinks'. I fear we made a mistake, working against our natural instincts in this way.

'You get to choose,' Edward says when he comes back to bed, an hour or so later, perhaps longer, after singing Will to sleep with a lullaby I have never heard before, but which made my toes curl with its sweetness. 'Either you commit to what we're doing, or it's over. All of it.'

What are Edward's eyes doing? The lids are red and the pupils contracting as he stares at me, his chin trembling. I look away and he snaps his fingers in my face to make me turn back. I have never seen such violence from my husband.

'Don't do that. That's not the kind of thing we do to each other.'

'Listen to me,' he says, his voice breaking. 'We are doing this together or there is no more we.'

'And if I can't?'

'You must try. And now it's your turn to apologize to Romeo.'

'I cannot call him by that name.'

'But that's his name! He's too old to change it. After all he's been through, we cannot now call him Will. He must be Romeo.'

'It's not a name I can say. It's too ridiculous. It makes me feel like the Juliet I am not.'

'Then what could you call him? Just as a start.'

I think about this, try to judge from his expression whether Edward really means what he says, but there is determination there, no flicker of falseness. He sounds like he is trying to be patient with me, despite whatever he feels. What would I do to save *us*? Embrace a beast in our home? Isn't there a folk tale of a monkey turning human? I can think only of stories – real ones – of orphan children raised by baboons and eventually saved by human society. The retraining, the unmonkeying of those human apes, sometimes takes years, as the evolution of humans from our ape ancestors took countless millennia, I remind myself. I must adjust my expectations, perhaps every day for the rest of my life, decades spent in a mode of constant adjustment.

'I could call him *my boy*.'

'Then call him that at least. The name will come.'

'Or a nickname. I could call him a nickname. Something like Ro.'

Edward's eyes clear and he smiles despite his desire, I suspect, to be stern with me.

'You know what that means?' he asks.

'Enlighten me, o scholar of the arcane.'

'Rest. Repose. Peace. Noun or verb. A Germanic import. Perhaps originally Icelandic. *Ró*. As in the York Mystery Plays, which I was meant to be talking about today if you hadn't had your little kitchen drama. After God showed them round the garden, Adam said to Eve, "Nowe are we brought Bothe unto rest and ro." '

'Noun and verb? Imperative as well?'

'Not strictly, but I suppose it could be. Adjust its usage. Language is dynamic.'

'Name maketh man.'

Edward puts his hands on my shoulders and draws me close. 'We can but try.'

As I go to sleep, I think of the meaning of the child's whole name,

Romeo, an Italianization of the late Latin *Romaeus*, which meant one who makes pilgrimage to Rome, if I remember my high school Shakespeare class. Still, I cannot help feeling it is a vulgar name for a child today. Perhaps in Italy it would be different. Context is key. If I were to take him to Rome, to see the origins of his name, perhaps that would also, by some magic, *ro* him.

The next morning, I find the child again in front of the painting, this time standing on a chair, his face level with the canvas and square with the boy who is composed of fluid oil that has hardened into form: permanent, short of its destruction by fire or blade or the deteriorations of time. Does he see himself in that child with a tail? He has one hand on the wall to the left of the canvas, which is unframed, just as the artist intended, I believe, and as I found it in the gallery in Stellenbosch, in a room of the artist's other unframed canvases, blurred images of young men and women, families, one of a black nanny holding a screaming white infant titled 'Monster Love'. My heart drops when I see the child I am meant to love. I want to shout at him to get down, not to touch, but then remember my role. I am the one who says yes, Edward must say no. When the boy's right hand reaches up as if to touch the painting I know I cannot wait for my husband to get out of bed.

'It's better not to touch it,' I say. Romeo's head swivels so he can look at me, but his left hand remains stuck against the wall and the right one is frozen mid-reach. 'We have oil on our hands, and dirt, and those things are bad for art.'

'Why is oil bad for art?'

'It leaves a residue. A trace. An invisible mark. And over time, that trace would collect dust and dirt and gradually it would become a black mark, and over an even longer time that black mark would begin to decay and destroy the painting.'

He squints. I have lost him.

'Think of the painting as if it were the cleanest thing in the world. Would you want to get the cleanest thing in the world dirty?'

'Maybe.'

'But it's good to keep clean things clean.'

'You said it was okay for things to get dirty.'

'Some things, yes, but not works of art.'

'Why?'

'So we can enjoy them in their ideal state. So that other people can enjoy them. If we get a work of art that is very clean dirty, then it has to be cleaned again, and every time we clean it, a little bit of it gets worn down or disappears, and so we speed up its process of decay. This painting is in an almost ideal state. I acquired it – I bought it – new from a gallery. No one else has owned it but the artist herself. It is almost in its ideal state. It has never had to be cleaned. If we look after it, it will not have to be cleaned for a long time yet, and so we will make it last longer.'

'But I want to touch it. I want to see what it feels like.'

This is a boy, I realize, who has never touched an oil painting, who has never possessed anything of value other than his clothes and shoes and a few small toys.

'We'll get a special one just for you.'

'A painting?'

'Yes. We'll go today, to find a painting that you can touch.'

I tell Edward my plan and his eyes narrow, looking away from me in that English way he has of suggesting demurral, or deferral, I'm never sure which.

'How much will you spend?' he asks.

'A thousand. Fifteen hundred.'

'That much?'

'Not if I can help it,' I say, 'but that's what I'm prepared to spend to secure the future of the painting I love. The alternative is to frame it, under glass, and have it securely bolted to the wall, and that would cost no less.' I do not tell Edward, hardly tell myself, that I have dreamt of Romeo destroying it.

I take him to a junk shop that calls itself an Antiques Market.

Sensing his skittishness, I squeeze his hand, smiling with my eyes, as my mother taught me, to reassure, to express genuine warmth, although I feel the mechanics of my own performance. All too human.

The owner of the Market, a woman in her sixties, has an inflated sense of the stuff she peddles, thinking it all priceless when it is, mostly, run-of-the-mill brown furniture and Victorian genre paintings that few people want. She watches every move my boy makes.

'We're looking for a painting for my son's room,' I tell her. 'Something interesting, with character, with people in it.'

She leads us to the back of the shop and points to an antechamber full of paintings, some hanging, others stacked on the floor and leaning against the walls, many framed, a few not. I have in mind a classical scene, perhaps something with hunters, or even a family portrait. Romeo's eyes dart up and down before he shakes his head. 'It isn't here.'

'We haven't looked properly,' I say.

He dismisses pictures of horses and cows and dogs. He has no interest in a group portrait of one family's seven children. Landscapes bore him. Classical ruins puzzle him. 'Why make a painting of *that?*' If it has a frame, he shows no interest. Near the back of the room, I find a curious eighteenth-century painting of three men: a white Englishman, his son, and the man's African slave. I put it aside, but this is the one that Romeo notices.

'We could maybe take this one,' he says.

'But here's a nice tropical picture,' I say, finding a French salon painting of a woman with large breasts and a flowing white gown reclining on a divan surrounded by Asian-looking attendants. There is even a monkey playing on the ground, reaching for a bauble.

'No, this one,' Romeo insists, touching the picture of the three men. His index finger taps at its surface, while his ring and middle fingers scoot back and forth, learning the texture of varnish and oil, the suggestion of soft tackiness that remains, even years after a painting is finished.

In the end I buy both. The woman wraps them in brown paper and ties them up with a rough brown cord. We take a taxi home.

'It's a very gloomy painting,' Edward says, grimacing at the portrait of the three men, which now hangs above Romeo's bed.

'It's not *right*,' Romeo suddenly shouts, thrusting his fists to his side. I wonder if this is prompted by Edward's skepticism.

'But it's the one you wanted, my boy,' I remind him.

'I want the other one!' he screams.

I go to our bedroom and bring back the painting of the woman and the monkey and the Asian attendants. Louche, I think, a rather dubious painting for a little boy's room.

'No!' Romeo screams again. 'I want *your* painting. In *there*.' He points towards the living room. I know which painting he wants. It is time for Edward to play his part, to say no, to make the refusal palatable, but this time Romeo will not be consoled and we spend the rest of the day and the evening listening as he sobs in his room.

In the middle of the night, I wake from a deep but troubled sleep, *dream-ravaged*, I say to myself. Something has woken me, but Edward remains asleep. We went to bed to the sound of Romeo's cries slackening off. He refused to eat. He would not bathe. He went to bed in his day clothes. He screamed obscenities at us, worse than anything he said to George and Henry. For the first time in the past week, Edward looked shaken by the child's behavior. He saw what I have had the privilege, or burden, of seeing on my own.

'I don't know,' he said as we turned out the light. 'Perhaps you were right.'

I expect to find Romeo in the living room, but notice the light from his bedroom. When I look through the open door I am stunned to find *Interior: Monkeyboy* hanging above his bed, in place of the eighteenth-century portrait of the three men. He must have swapped the paintings on his own, and then I notice that he is wearing his new pajama bottoms but no shirt and his body is covered in red streaks.

At first I think he is bleeding, flayed, but then I see that on each of his arms there is only a red stripe of paint, watercolor, extending from his elbow to wrist, red stripes that imitate the red highlights on the arms of the boy in the painting. There is also an appendage, just above the waist of the pajamas at his back, a long thin tail, twisting slightly, that piece of rough brown cord from the Antiques Market, affixed to his skin with electrical tape.

For a moment we stand there, him looking at the picture, me looking at him from the hall. I hear the shushing of a bus and a siren's drone, although the noise is scarcely audible through the closed windows and may only be in my mind. Perhaps sensing my presence, Romeo turns his head, offering me a three-quarter view. His eyes are dark and beady, like those of the boy in the painting, his chin set with confidence, willfulness. Alpha, as George said. An alpha male, my Romeo. I know what I must do.

'Come here, my boy. We can dance if you like.'

'Now?'

'Yes. I am going to teach you to tango.' ■

SABINE

Jacob Aue Sobol

Introduction by Joanna Kavenna

In 1999, the Danish photographer Jacob Aue Sobol travelled to the small hunting community of Tiniteqilaaq, in south-eastern Greenland. He was twenty-three years old at the time, and intended to pass a few weeks photographing the inhabitants. Then, as often happens, reality altered around him, and he fell deeply in love with a nineteen-year-old local woman called Sabine. He returned to Tiniteqilaaq and stayed for two years, hunting and fishing, and for a while he couldn't photograph anything at all. Yet, gradually, he began to create a series of extraordinary portraits of the Arctic wilderness and the intimacies of love.

In Greenland, the ice cap haunts you all the time – a vast expanse, lingering at the edge of vision. Ice covers 80 per cent of the island. In places, it is over three kilometres thick, and more than 100,000 years old. The Greenlanders live along the coast, on tracts of moraine rubble by the fjords and mountains. Icebergs drift slowly past, silent fleets of them, some striped blue and white, others stained the darkening blue of dusk. The ice is sonorous, and communicative: it creaks, and groans. The rocks are covered with delicate, variegated flowers, in red, yellow and orange. There are Arctic hares so large they resemble humans wearing costumes, like a practical joke. The sky above changes constantly – one moment it is pink, then purple, then, abruptly, everything – the ocean, the sky, your hands – turn silver, and you fear you have lost your wits entirely. Darkness falls and the Northern Lights pulse across the curved hallucinogenic heavens. There are significant hardships of daily life as well – violent storms, the *piteraqs*, coil around the wooden houses, winds screaming like lunatics; the grinding poverty of many Greenlanders – and all the time you sense the eerie presence of the ice cap above, haunting the settlements and crushing the land.

Sobol's photographs beautifully evoke the grandeur and severity of this region – the misty silvery ocean, the mesmerising strangeness of the Arctic night. In one photograph, a sombre group convenes for a cold burial. In another, the blurred sky is full of stars, flickering lights or snow. A fishing net fans out across the whiteness; the corpse of a seal is dragged away for flensing; a silhouetted figure balances upon the frozen ocean. The lapping of the waves, the cries of birds. The steady dispersal of ice. Sobol brilliantly captures the confounding aspects of this place, where you are wild with the exquisite loveliness of everything, and then, suddenly, appalled and perplexed by the surrounding immensity. You understand, entirely, at such moments, why shamanic rituals in the Arctic commune with shadows, the spirits of the dead; why the self is not envisaged as composite and material but might convey alter-selves, ethereal emissaries, across the ice. In one photograph, a boy seems to fly off the balcony of a house; elsewhere, two indeterminate figures move through prevailing nothingness. In one particularly striking image we see a hunter and his dogs, progressing into whiteness. The print resembles a silvered daguerreotype in an antiquarian journal – the boundaries between past and present are blurred, as are the distinctions between land, sea and sky.

Yet, in many of the photos we are inside, and Sobol's camera is focused on his lover, Sabine. We see her lying on a bed, or standing at a window, a view of snow-striped rocks beyond. She is by turns weary and playful; she sleeps, washes, smiles; she is blithe and reticent. She is often photographed without clothes; Sobol seems to contrast her nakedness with the swaddled humans outside, their features obscured. Traditionally, Inuit men and women would remove all their clothing when inside their houses, observing a practical distinction between gelid exterior and warm interior. Sabine's nakedness is less erotic than matter of fact; the atmosphere of the portraits is loving and conspiratorial. Sobol ventures into a storm-blasted Arctic region, and at first he is quite desperate, he doesn't know if he can endure the isolation. The elements are overwhelming. Humans appear as shadows, dark traces, bleakly opposed to the prevailing whiteness. Then – his wooden house becomes an everywhere, to paraphrase an old poem, and Sobol invokes the boundless remit of his beloved. This is a wonderful series of intimate portraits and dreamlike panoramas, celebrating the finite lives of individuals and the strange limitless beauty of the North. ∎

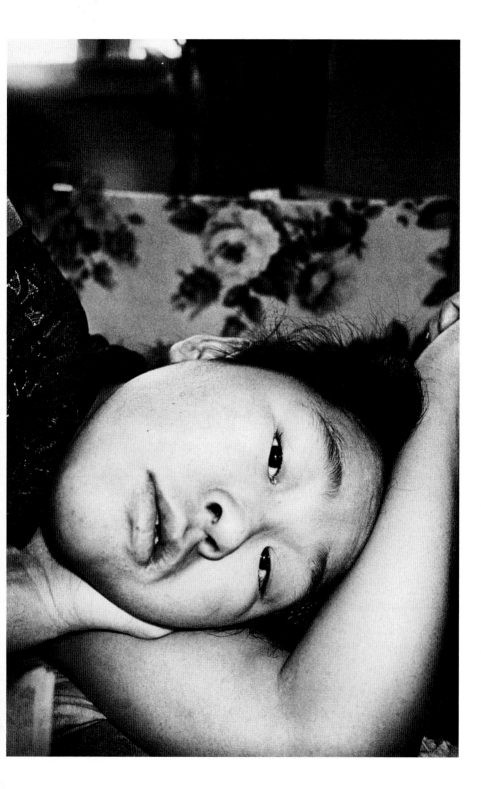

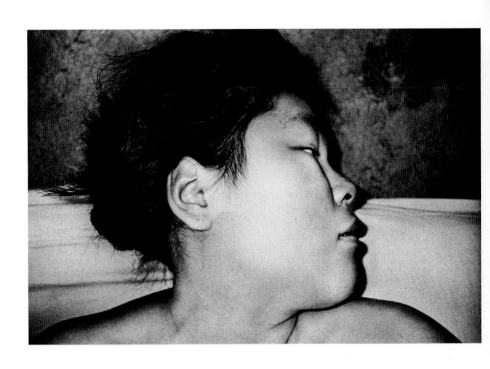

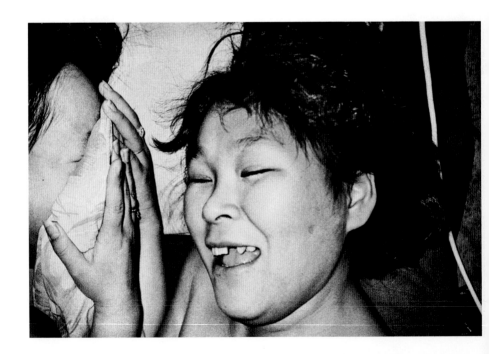

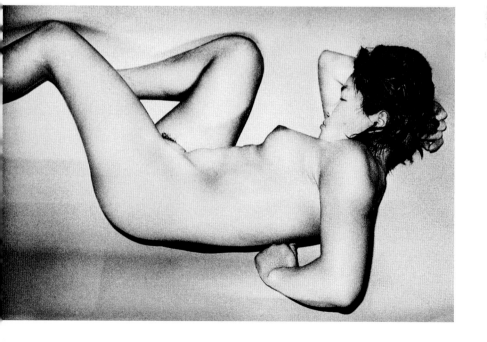

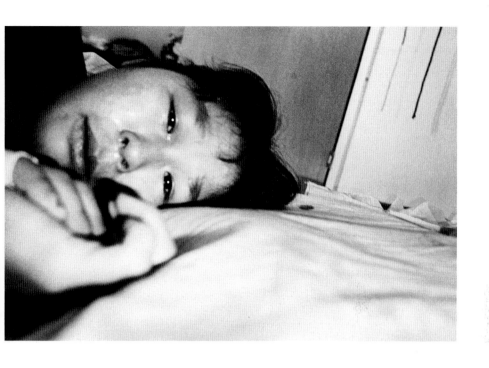

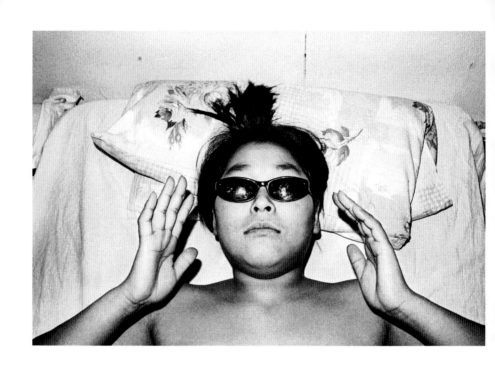

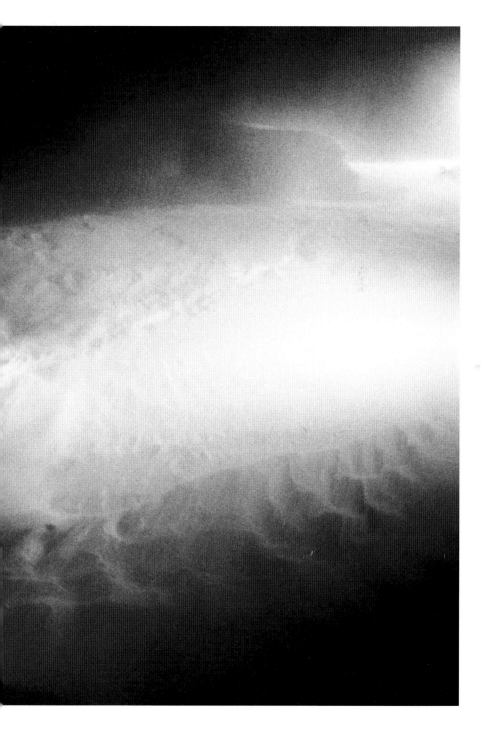

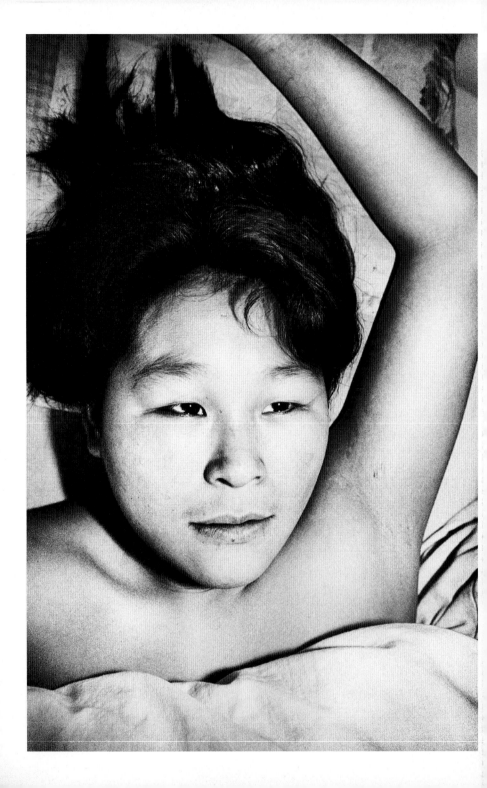

GRANTA

THE MAGAZINE OF NEW WRITING

PRINT SUBSCRIPTION REPLY FORM FOR UK, EUROPE
AND REST OF THE WORLD (includes digital and app access).
For digital-only subscriptions, please visit granta.com/subscriptions.

GUARANTEE: If I am ever dissatisfied with my *Granta* subscription, I will simply notify you, and you will send me a complete refund or credit my credit card, as applicable, for all un-mailed issues.

YOUR DETAILS

TITLE ....
NAME ....
ADDRESS ....
POSTCODE ....
EMAIL ....

☐ Please tick this box if you do not wish to receive special offers from *Granta*
☐ Please tick this box if you do not wish to receive offers from organisations selected by *Granta*

YOUR PAYMENT DETAILS

1) ☐ Pay £32 (saving £20) by direct debit.

   To pay by direct debit please complete the mandate and return to the address shown below.

2) Pay by cheque or credit/debit card. Please complete below:

   1 year subscription: ☐ UK: £36   ☐ Europe: £42   ☐ Rest of World: £46

   3 year subscription: ☐ UK: £99   ☐ Europe: £108   ☐ Rest of World: £126

   I wish to pay by ☐ CHEQUE ☐ CREDIT/DEBIT CARD

   Cheque enclosed for £_____ made payable to *Granta*.

   Please charge £ _____ to my: ☐ Visa ☐ MasterCard ☐ Amex ☐ Switch/Maestro

   Card No. ☐☐☐☐☐☐☐☐☐☐☐☐☐☐☐☐☐☐

   Valid from *(if applicable)* ☐☐ / ☐☐   Expiry Date ☐☐ / ☐☐   Issue No. ☐☐

   Security No. ☐☐☐

SIGNATURE .... DATE ....

Instructions to your Bank or Building Society to pay by direct debit

BANK NAME ....
BANK ADDRESS ....
POSTCODE ....
ACCOUNT IN THE NAMES(S) OF: ....
SIGNED .... DATE ....

DIRECT Debit

Instructions to your Bank or Building Society: Please pay Granta Publications direct debits from the account detailed on this instruction subject to the safeguards assured by the direct debit guarantee. I understand that this instruction may remain with Granta and, if so, details will be passed electronically to my bank/building society. Banks and building societies may not accept direct debit instructions from some types of account.

Bank/building society account number
☐☐☐☐☐☐☐☐

Sort Code
☐☐ ☐☐ ☐☐

Originator's Identification
9 1 3 1 3 3

Please mail this order form with payment instructions to:

Granta Publications
12 Addison Avenue
London, W11 4QR
Or call +44(0)208 955 7011 Or visit
GRANTA.COM/SUBSCRIPTIONS for details

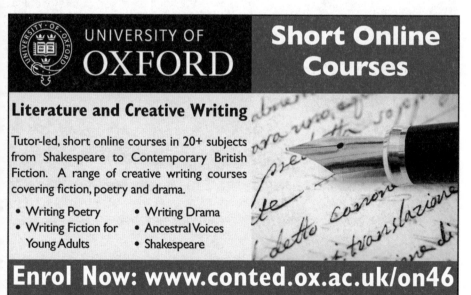

Mountains and Valleys, c. 1933–1935
Indianapolis Museum of Art, gift of the Eiteljorg Museum of American Indians and Western Art

THE TENANT

Victor Lodato

hen Marie saw the small house, nestled almost invisibly among weedy hills and sycamores, she thought, *jackpot*. She thought, *heaven*.

Hell, she thought, *I could live and die here*.

Of course, all she said to the McGregors was, 'It'll do.'

The McGregors owned the property and lived in the large house next door – though *next door* was a relative term; the main house was at least a hundred yards away. Through the trees all Marie could see of it was a patch of pale blue siding – which, in the right mood, she could easily pretend was part of the sky.

The right mood was not uncommon lately. It often involved gin. Marie was careful not to put the empties in the recycling bin. She didn't wish to give the McGregors the wrong idea. There was something distinctly Christiany about them. Something to do with how polite they were – a politeness that seemed a bit performative, as if they were trying to make a good impression, not only on her, but on someone off in the wings. Marie often had the urge to look behind her to see who they were talking to. It was nerve-wracking – though surely it was worse for them. Believing in God was no doubt stressful, like living under constant surveillance.

Marie was grateful for her freedom. And, lately, she'd become intrigued by the idea of something more. Anonymity. It seemed a very classy business card: cloud-white and completely blank. She'd hand them out to anyone who got too close.

Luckily the McGregors hadn't asked her to fill out one of those renter-information packets, or done a credit check. They'd been satisfied with her offer to pay the first six months in advance.

As soon as Marie signed the lease, she felt a weight lifted from her heart. Maybe this lightness had something to do with the land and the trees, which reminded her of the estate she'd grown up on, across the valley, in the Rincons.

Not that she'd been particularly happy there – but it was *childhood* and so, at a certain age, revered. And certainly it hadn't been terrible. Her parents had been decent people – though they'd had their edges, their sorrows. Their moods had oppressed her as a child, but now she saw it as a good sign, a sign that perhaps they'd wanted more than what they'd had. When they died five years ago on the highway, it had been their first trip out of Tucson in twenty years. They were going to Apache County to see the ruins, but made it only as far as Pinetop. A sleep-deprived trucker carrying a load of frozen fruit had swerved and toppled.

'Blueberries everywhere,' one witness had said.

The caskets had been closed.

The first month at the rental, Marie slept better than she had in a while. It was quiet, and the McGregors kept their distance. She'd told them she was a writer; she needed her privacy. The lie had come out of her with such ease that she wondered if maybe she *should* write a book. Now that she'd stopped dating, she could do with a new hobby.

Mostly she read – and when she got up to look out the large front window, it was nice to occasionally see the animals. The McGregors had four piebald cows and a scattering of Buckeye chickens. Before renting the place, Marie had been asked if it was all right if the animals grazed, as they always had, on the entire property. Not at all, she'd said – let them roam.

Of course, she hadn't considered the shit – which, for weeks now, had been accumulating on what she thought of as *her* part of the land, though there was no fence to mark such distinctions. More than once, Marie had been wandering about the hills, musing on something she'd read, only to land disastrously in some fresh excretion. The cows were particularly prodigious, leaving behind mounds the size of Bundt cakes.

In addition to the shit, she hadn't thought about children. One afternoon a girl appeared – a preschoolish type called *Lacy*, who, in violation of her name, was indelicate and wild, chunky, and most disturbingly, a shouter. She often darted about, in white sneakers, on some manic escapade. Apparently she had a sixth sense about how to avoid the excrement. Her white sneakers remained pristine. When she leapt across the hills, it was as if she were preparing for flight. Her shouts had the shrill urgency of a crow.

All in all, though, it wasn't really a crisis – more of a nuisance. Neither the animals nor the girl ever came right up to the house. Still, after Marie had been there nearly three months, she wondered if she might talk to the McGregors about the possibility of a fence. Maybe just a little one around the rental house. She'd even be willing to share the cost.

But how to start such a conversation? Especially since she hardly ever spoke with the owners. Perhaps she'd say it was an aesthetic thing – not mention the child or the animals. A fence, she could say, would add to a feeling of home. She'd play up the romance of it. White picket sort of nonsense.

The funny thing was: despite the problems, she was settling in nicely here. What she'd felt on first seeing the place – that this was somewhere she might stay awhile – she felt still.

Plus, it wasn't easy to find furnished rentals in Tucson. All Marie carried now were three suitcases, and she had no intention of acquiring anything else. Other people's beds and dressers suited her just fine. The McGregors' cottage had a yellow Formica table that at first had made her wince, but now was a happy revelation each morning when she woke to it buttered in sunlight. Drinking coffee there seemed right, seemed familiar.

Careful, she thought.

Because it was frightening, really, how quickly a person got used to things. Attachment was an octopus. Even when you cut off its arms, they grew back. You had to keep a knife in your back pocket. This was her ninth rental in five years.

Marie sighed. She knew the drill. She might allow herself a few more months here – but then it would be time to move.

When her parents died, Marie had been living in Phoenix – had been living there for nearly twelve years. That former life seemed a blur now: a job at an art gallery, a two-story townhouse, a tall man with a beard who'd stayed with her most nights and who she'd assumed she'd eventually marry.

After the accident, though, she'd come to Tucson to attend to her parents' affairs, taking a leave from the gallery and telling the man that she'd be back in a few weeks.

She stayed for six months – the whole time in her parents' house, the house of her childhood, the house that she, as sole heir, had inherited. Her mother's dog was still around, a chocolate Lab, old and infirm now. It pained Marie to watch him limp and collapse, often at her feet, looking up as if there was something she could do. She fed him green beans from a can, his favorite, but eventually he stopped taking food. When the vet said it might be soon, Marie didn't hesitate: she put the dog to sleep.

It'd been the last bit of business. Still, she'd stayed on at the old place – wondering if she might invite the bearded man to live with her; he'd been down to visit several times and commented how much he liked the house. He'd also mentioned something about the two of them starting their life. 'Time to get to it,' he'd said. But the more Marie had thought about this phrase, the more it had rankled her. What was the man implying – that she was running out of time? What was she then? Thirty-nine?

Marie never invited him down again, and soon after, she began dating other men – brief affairs, usually less than a week. The sex was always conducted in her parents' bedroom. Marie felt like a spider, taking the men apart on her mother's best satin sheets. The orgasms often ended in tears, but they were glorious. Though Marie wasn't religious in any way, or inclined toward metaphysics, she had a sense that there was some higher purpose to these sexual encounters. She sensed somehow that she was feeding the dead. Giving them something for the road. Something better than cold blueberries.

Her parents had rarely touched her as a child – rarely touched each other. When the men left, Marie shuffled from room to room, sorting through her parents' stuff. They'd been hoarders of a sort. The nights she spent alone in the house, she often felt sick. It might have been her diet (green apples and cans of sardines). More likely it was the exhaustion of grief, which had been a full-time job back then.

Slowly, she'd got rid of almost everything. Every piece of furniture, all her mother's jewelry, her father's collection of Western art. She even sold the most valuable paintings – the small Dixon of a crazy sky chockablock with clouds, and the good-sized Blumenschein of a stoic Navaho draped in bright blankets and gesturing like some Martha Graham princess. *I offer peace* – or something to that effect.

As a child, she'd loved the paintings, hanging in every room like an extra window: desert landscapes of muted colors, as if recalled from a dream; horses and riders kicking up dust under blue moonbeams; women patting tortillas outside adobes pinked with sunset. She'd stood before these paintings with her father, who'd explained how they preserved a history of light, how the light was different back then, before the cities were built. Romantic, surely, he'd said, but important, historical. Marie had wanted to live in that light; imagined that she'd become a painter one day.

Why had she told the McGregors she was a writer? Only now did she see that she could have offered a much more truthful lie.

For a while she completely forgot about the idea of a fence. But then summer came and the girl had friends and the animals had flies that were always getting into the house. She walked over to the McGregors' with some apple cookies.

A boy answered the door. Older than the girl, probably around fourteen. Horsey-looking, but in an attractive sort of way. Marie was horsey herself. *Handsome,* her mother had always called her.

'Are your parents home?'

The boy stared dully, as if woken from a nap. 'They're at work.'

Marie glanced at her watch; it was nearly six. 'Long day, huh?'

The boy grimaced. He seemed a bit slow.

'I'm the renter. Next door,' she said, in case he wasn't up to speed.

'I know. I seen you.'

Marie smiled. She'd put the cookies on a ceramic platter; it was a bit heavy.

'You don't work?' the boy said.

'No,' replied Marie. 'May I give you this?'

'What is it?'

A piece of cow shit, she wanted to say. 'Cookies,' she told him. 'I made cookies.'

'Oh.' He immediately took them and peeled back the tinfoil. 'Can I eat one?'

'That is their purpose.'

He took a bite, said it was pretty good.

Marie chucked up another smile. 'Maybe I could wait until your folks get home?'

The boy nodded, backed away from the door.

The house was a mess. When Marie walked in, she stepped on what might have been a piece of breakfast cereal. The sofa was piled with clothing. Open textbooks were scattered across a coffee table.

'Doing your homework?'

'I guess.'

The boy was as blank as the walls, which contained no decoration whatsoever. No mirrors or shelves of knickknacks, no paintings. The furnishings were a mishmash, and badly arranged. It all seemed very provisional.

Maybe they'd bought the house only recently. Marie realized she knew nothing about the family.

'Have you lived here a long time?'

'Forever,' the boy said. He was on his second cookie.

The house was hot, and Marie untwirled the silk scarf from around her neck.

'So, are you, like, rich?' the boy asked.

What a question, thought Marie. She was renting a shoebox from this idiot's parents. 'Yes,' she said. 'I'm loaded.'

The kid nodded, munched. He was liable to finish the whole plate before his parents got home, lessening the effect of the gesture. She couldn't begin a conversation about a fence with a present of crumbs.

'You know what? I think I'll come back another time. Maybe save some cookies for your sister?' suggested Marie.

The boy stopped mid-chew. 'Oh, I thought . . . Sorry.'

'No.' Marie blushed. 'Eat as many as you like. I can bring more.'

The boy said he liked chocolate-chip best, and second-best, oatmeal.

'Yes, well, we'll see. No promises.' She paused at the door. 'You know, there's a lot of poop outside my house.'

'The cows,' the boy said unhelpfully. 'We got it, too.'

'I would imagine so. I was just wondering if maybe someone could scoop it.'

'Don't need to be scooped. It's good for it to stay there.'

'Good for what?'

'I don't know. For like the grass and stuff, I guess. I'll tell my dad.'

'Thank you.'

'Uh-huh,' the boy mumbled, turning back to his books.

Marie watched him. Terrible posture, a paper-thin tee stretched over the bow of his spine.

He looked up. 'You know, my grandmother was supposed to live there, where you're living.'

'Really,' said Marie. 'Could she not afford the rent?'

'What? No,' the boy said. 'She died.'

Marie adjusted her scarf. 'Well, that's . . . were you close to her?'

'Nah. She wasn't from around here. Plus, she was pretty old. She had to put, like, oxygen on her face and everything.'

Marie widened her eyes. 'Wow.'

'I know,' said the boy.

'Well, I'll be going,' said Marie. 'No need to tell your parents I was here.'

'They're gonna figure it out.' He gestured toward the cookies.

Marie sighed. 'Why don't you just . . .' She marched toward the couch and slid the remaining cookies onto a piece of the boy's notebook paper, then took back the platter. 'It'll be our secret.'

'Should I tell them about the cow shit?' he asked.

Marie glanced at the dirty carpet and said it wasn't necessary, she'd give his parents a ring.

On the way back, she wanted to scream.

Or gag. *Grandma*'s house? And here she was, baking cookies for these people. When they should be attending to *her* needs.

That was the whole point of renting, was it not? You were supposed to have no concerns, no responsibilities. Landlords were the parents, renters the children. Not that Marie wanted to get familial about it; it was just a metaphor.

I like chocolate-chip best! Well, he could go fuck himself.

It was nearly sunset when Marie stepped onto her porch. She checked her shoes for muck before entering the house and then made some lemonade.

It wasn't *exactly* lemonade, but that's what she called it, should anyone ask. She put it in a thermos, added some ice cubes, and grabbed the car keys. She needed to be outside, closer to the mountains. The mountains always put things in perspective for her – made the smallness, the crushability of humans, seem valid.

The McGregors' place was near the Tortolitas – dreary jagged peaks with no water to speak of. Wild pigs and petroglyphs, the ruins of Honey Bee Village. The Hohokam were long gone, but their ancestors, the Tohono O'odham, lingered on, sick with sugar. Half of them had diabetes. No one painted these Indians. They were too fat.

Marie had briefly dated a native boy in high school, and for nearly a year she'd been mocked – accused of a fondness for Tohono O'odham scrotum. Her parents hadn't approved either. 'You can do better,' her mother had chided.

He was a sweet boy, a bit of a punk, with long shiny hair that smelled like bubblegum. *Albert.* She'd gone with him once to San Xavier and they'd eaten fry bread, wandered stoned through the Mission. They'd only kissed, fondled through cloth. Virgins, both of them. She'd never seen his scrotum.

Marie sipped her lemonade and drove toward Sanctuary Cove, where the land stumbled upward into craggy cliffs. It was easy to imagine flying into oblivion here – her old Volvo sprouting wings and sailing into the sainted blue. She parked at the trailhead and kept her eyes on the rocks, avoiding the development visible to her right – a vast beehive of red-tiled roofs where there used to be ranches and cotton fields.

This was the northern edge of the city. It would have been a breeze to hop on the freeway and drive away from Tucson. But every time she tried this, she found herself blocked – not by mountains or traffic or flash floods, but by something in her blood. It was as if she lived in some crazy psychic zoo, a woman trapped behind invisible walls of glass.

Marie wondered what held her here. It wasn't as if she thought she'd see them again. She barely expected to see herself. The light had changed too much.

Still, it was home – more than Phoenix had ever been. Marie kicked at some agate shards and wondered who was living in her townhouse. She'd never met the new owners. After selling her parents' home, she'd put the Phoenix place on the market. She'd done well on both. Add to that the paintings, the jewelry, the insurance payouts – yes, she was what that stupid McGregor boy would call rich. She should show him the suitcase one day, blow his dimwit mind.

Honestly, though, it was a burden. Most people had no idea how much a suitcase stuffed with cash weighed.

Ha! She was drunk enough to laugh at herself. A rich woman complaining about her pearls: they're *so* heavy.

Marie took off her scarf – one of her last good accessories – and let it go into a rising wind. Sometimes the invisible could be your friend. She watched the scarf fly up – a miracle, really – the purple streak of silk blending perfectly into the sunset.

More, more, she thought. She took off her sandals and threw them toward a dried-up ocotillo. One hooked near the top, bending a stalk like an overweight angel on a Christmas tree.

H er head hurt quite a bit. Every morning it was like this. Weeks passed in a kind of stutter: not every moment was there. She felt as if she were hopping between stones, but unaware of the hop – only the stone: a hard landing that jarred her skull.

One morning she woke splayed out on the floor with her head in a suitcase. It was half filled with clothing, and so in some sense a legitimate pillow. The question was: was she leaving or not?

She often found herself packing, but only in a half-hearted, desultory sort of way.

It was still summer, and changing residence during the summer was horrible. The temperature was steadfastly in the hundreds now, and even in the best rentals she'd be able to smell the previous tenants, catch glimpses of their sins. Too much light, too much heat – it exposed everything. Maybe she'd wait until August. Hopefully the monsoons would come and bring some air one could actually move through with purpose.

Summer was a time for stillness. The little house had peppy AC, and so other than runs to the grocery store Marie stayed inside. Her books came by post. She was rereading the Russians. The text, though, was ridiculously small, and since it hurt her pride to wear reading glasses, she ordered some large-print editions. *Anna Karenina* alone arrived in five volumes and was nearly two thousand pages. Reading it was a revelation – the oversized text making the book seem like a story for children, and for this reason all the more shocking. The sentences practically slapped you in the face, welcomed you afresh to the world of humans. The letters no longer ants, but ladybugs – the *O*s large enough to catch Marie's tears.

Sometimes she stood at the window and waved to the animals. They never waved back. Maybe they were afraid of her hair. It had grown quite a bit in the past few months, and she rarely combed it. There were butter blotches on all her T-shirts.

At least she kept the house clean – and this allowed her some degree of good opinion about herself. She was an excellent tenant. Even when she vacated a place in the middle of the night, she left it immaculate – the toilet scrubbed, the sinks spotless. She was always paid-up, and often left a little something extra.

Marie set early October as her departure date from the McGregors'. Until then, she'd read, sketch, drink her coffee at the yellow table. *Yes,* she reminded herself: she was sketching again. It was surely a good sign – though what she rendered in her little pads were no more than nervous doodles, swoops and swirls, a mindless sort of art, free of logic or ambition. Marie often did it for hours, forgetting lunch. In the evening, she cooked elaborate meals – and, despite the heat, baked a new dessert every few days.

Among the few possessions she'd kept were her mother's recipe cards. She looked through them, here at the McGregors', and in mid-July enjoyed Christmas cookies and rum cake. She made a lot of puddings, as well, to use up the eggs. Every week, someone left a large basket of them outside her door – though the culprit was stealthy, making the delivery before dawn. Mrs McGregor probably, doing her Christian duty. Eggs for the spinster.

When Marie opened the suitcase that contained the recipes, it was the first time she'd done so since she'd zipped it shut on a balmy

January day nearly half a decade before. She wouldn't have been surprised to find the suitcase full of ashes or frozen fruit – like some gag prize on that game show her mother used to watch.

No such luck, though: the case had kept its treasure. She sat on the rented bed and looked through some of the relics. A photo of her parents – her father in a snazzy shirt with lapels the size of pizza slices, and her mother in a dress that looked exactly like whipped cream. Their faces glowed – though that was probably a trick of longing, some lie the living told about the dead.

Anyway, what Marie liked best about the photo wasn't the youthful beauty of her parents, but their stance, leaning against each other like they'd had one too many. They looked cheap and wild and happy. It made her feel lonely for a version of them she'd never known. For most of her life they'd been brittle and distant – generous with their wisdom, though, which usually seemed to be a story about how even amidst comfort and success the best of life was always behind you. Her grandparents, who'd lived on an old pony ranch on the Rillito, had radiated a similar wisdom. Sadness ran in the family like an eternal spring. Marie was awake to it now, the cold water coursing through her blood. This time of year, it was almost refreshing.

One morning, she stumbled outside to find another basket of eggs – and instead of taking them inside, she threw them, one by one, against a tree. The following week there was no delivery. Even the chickens kept their distance.

Emptiness. That was the reckoning of summer.

The little girl, too, seemed to have vanished. Probably it was too hot for her to be flailing about outside. She was no doubt lying in a torpor on the dirty carpet, eating from a box of breakfast cereal.

Marie sort of missed her, and sometimes on her midnight strolls she wandered across the imaginary line she'd set that separated the McGregors' property from hers. She got close enough to hear their voices. Sometimes she heard screams, sometimes gunshots – though that was probably just the television.

The knock was a box being nailed shut – a box she was trapped inside.

Then the knock was a bird against the glass.

Then it was a fist.

Marie woke to the McGregor boy standing behind the window, grimacing. She pulled up the sheets in case she was naked.

'I'll come around the front,' he shouted.

When she opened the door, dressed to kill in a moth-eaten serape, the boy said he was here for the pies.

'I haven't made any,' said Marie.

'No, I mean, I just thought I'd pick them up,' he persisted.

Marie felt slightly dizzy. She flattened down her hair and asked the boy what the hell he was talking about.

'The cow shit,' he said. 'I brought a bucket.' He held it up.

She stared at him a while before saying, 'Well, you certainly waited long enough.'

He shrugged. 'Been busy.'

Marie understood the correct phrase was, 'Thank you for coming,' but instead she said, 'I don't think one bucket's going to cut it.'

The boy said it would if he smashed it down. 'Plus I ain't gonna do all of it, just where it's bothering you.'

'And where is that?' asked Marie.

'I suppose where you can see it?' he said.

Fair enough, thought Marie – and though she had no more to say, she lingered at the door.

The boy looked down and coughed. 'Well, I better get started before it hots up.'

She watched him from the window. He'd brought a filthy shovel, which he'd set against the egg-plastered tree. Out on the weedy hills he scooped and dumped in a white T-shirt that slowly soaked through. Marie peeked at the clock (*8.40*) and then at the thermometer on the porch (*92*).

The boy scanned the ground, bleary without sunglasses.

He wiped his eyes, marching from pie to pie. Sometimes he didn't scoop the shit, but only crushed it with his foot and then mashed the dry bits into the earth. His boots were as big as a man's, and though he was skinny, he had a man's seriousness. He worked as if someone's life depended on it. When he saw Marie staring at him from the window, he waved. Marie backed away and faded into the house.

I'll give him a tip, she thought.

Though perhaps it was better to give him nothing. He was doing no more than basic upkeep, which was the owner's responsibility. Marie went to her bedroom and looked in the mirror. She was wearing the same clothes as the day before – a linen blouse so wrinkled from sleeping in it that it looked like the skin of an elephant.

After changing her outfit, she went back to the window. The boy was gone, and for a moment she panicked – a feeling that confused her. Then she saw him galumphing back from the main house with a wheelbarrow. He stationed himself on another hill and resumed his labor. When he took off his shirt, exposing a shockingly white chest, Marie winced. The poor kid was going to fry.

Marie's mother had been pale, too, and had so feared the sun that she'd slathered on protective creams that made her even whiter. She'd often left the house looking like some kabuki empress. Living in the desert wasn't for everyone. You had to be tough.

Marie shut the curtains and lay on the couch. Volume two of *Anna Karenina*, a fat paperback, curled on the coffee table. She fetched it, and despite the dimness of the closed-up room, didn't bother to turn on a lamp. Another good thing about these large-print books was that you could practically read them in the dark – which, as far as Marie was concerned, was the perfect way to read Tolstoy.

When the knock came, she refused to get up. 'All done?' she shouted.

'Yup!' came the reply.

'Thank you!' chirped Marie – and when she didn't hear his boots moving away, she sighed and checked her pockets for cash. 'One second!'

His face was flushed and his shoulders pink. 'I got most of it, I think.'

Marie had the money in her closed fist. It was to be a gift and not an obligation. She waited to get a reading on the boy's greed. She could smell his boots. He seemed reluctant to speak.

'Yes?' said Marie.

'Yeah, I was just, uh . . . I was supposed to ask if maybe you wanted to come over for dinner sometime.'

Marie was speechless.

'My mom said sorry if she was rude about the eggs, she shoulda asked you if you wanted them. She said you could come on Friday or Saturday.'

'This week won't work,' said Marie. 'But tell your mother thank you.'

'Sure. My dad already told her you wouldn't come.'

When Marie said she was sorry, the boy shrugged. 'I wouldn't go either, if they invited me.'

Marie wasn't sure what to do with this information, but decided to defuse the confession with wit. 'But you *have* to go,' she said. '*You* are their prisoner.'

The boy laughed and said he sure was.

And then he told her his name was Harland.

'Well, Harland, maybe you'd like to come by in a week or so and clean up again.'

'I could, yes. If you want.'

'I do.' Marie extended her hand and opened her fist. It felt perverse, giving the kid a hundred-dollar bill – but it felt wonderful, too.

'Oh,' said Harland. 'I don't – I don't have any change.'

'I don't want change,' said Marie. 'You worked hard.'

He was still staring at the bill as she shut the door.

The next time he came, there was little to do. After he scooped the pies, he gathered some dead brush, then scattered grass seeds on a balding hill.

Marie sat on the porch, reading.

'Do you always carry seeds in your pocket?' she asked him.

'Not to school,' he said. 'But around here it comes in handy.'

He was charmingly literal. If Marie was ever sarcastic or unkind, it seemed to go right over the boy's head. She found it best to keep things simple, though this was surprisingly hard. Simplicity was a kind of honesty, and Marie was out of practice.

'Would you like something to drink, Harland?'

'No, thank you,' he said – and then: 'Well, what are *you* drinking?'

'Oh, this is just . . .' Marie made a discouraging face. 'This is just lemonade.'

When Harland said he'd take some of that, Marie said she'd just poured the last of it. 'How about some milk?'

'Milk's good,' he said. 'If it's cold.'

He removed his boots at the door and came inside wearing grubby sweat socks. The way he kept one foot atop the other, Marie suspected he was hiding a hole.

'Would you like to sit down? Cool off?'

He shook his head. 'I need to do some things for my dad.'

She handed him a glass of milk and a brownie, which he ate quickly, nodding in approval.

Marie had the money in her pocket, but she waited. 'Would you like another one?'

'I don't wanna be a pig,' said Harland.

'*Please.* I've already eaten five today.'

The boy approached the table and Marie pushed the plate of brownies closer to him. As he chewed, he looked around the room. There was no wall between the kitchen and the living area. Marie was glad the place was neat; no doubt the boy would be submitting a report.

'You sure got a lot of books.'

'Passes the time.'

'I guess,' said Harland. 'Do you use that chair?' He pointed toward the plaid-upholstered La-Z-Boy near the television.

Marie said, yes, sometimes she did.

'That used to be my chair. I used to come over here all the time before you moved in. After my dad built it for my grandma, there was, like, almost a year before you showed up. So it was kinda my house for a while.'

'Well, I won't be here forever,' said Marie.

Harland said he didn't think she would be. He walked over to his chair. 'You see all these cuts?'

'I was wondering about those.' The arms were covered with gashes, inside of which you could see the white stuffing.

'I made them,' said Harland.

'Did you?'

He nodded and sat down. 'With my pocketknife. Which I lost, by the way. So if you find it . . .'

He didn't say anything after that – only caressed the distressed fabric and stared at the wall with slightly raised eyes. Marie was tempted to grab her sketchpad in an attempt to capture what she was seeing, which seemed to be a face of exquisite beauty. Something about the tightly locked brow gave the impression of an animal preparing to pounce. It was some time before she realized that the boy was crying.

'I'm not,' he said before Marie had uttered a word. 'I just got some of that shit in my eyes.'

Marie pretended to believe him and turned away to pour herself more lemonade. She took a few swigs before speaking. 'I haven't seen your sister in a while.'

'Yeah, she was in some trouble,' grumbled Harland. 'She broke something.'

Marie asked if it was something valuable, and Harland said he guessed so, it was her ankle. 'Cast came off last week, but now she has to go to, like, resuscitation.'

'You mean, rehabilitation?'

'Something like that. I ain't got the greatest memory.'

'You also have terrible grammar,' said Marie. 'We really should work on that.'

When she sat on the couch – nearly a stumble – she saw that he'd pulled some of the stuffing from one of the gashes on the armchair. It looked like a tiny puff of smoke. He continued to tug at it until he'd made a miniature tornado. Marie stared at it, mesmerized.

'Stop,' she said. 'Don't make it worse.'

She was fading. It was a struggle to stay upright.

'I have to go,' said Harland.

'Me too,' mumbled Marie.

As the boy stood, she pushed the money into his hand.

He quickly checked the amount – and this time he didn't bring up the matter of change. 'All right then. See ya.'

He didn't come the next week. Marie, expecting him, had made gingerbread. She'd also stitched up the armchair with a sewing kit she'd found in one of the drawers. She couldn't remember the last time she'd used a needle and thread. Her mother had certainly never sewn anything. As a child, if Marie ever ripped a shirt or a dress, it went right in the trash, or was cut into rags for the housekeeper.

It was satisfying work, stuffing the stray batting back inside the arms and closing the gashes with black thread. It gave Marie a sense of accomplishment. To have saved something that was essentially worthless – the impulse was almost religious.

Possibly she'd been overzealous, though, and put in too many stitches. The chair looked sort of gruesome now.

'I had to operate,' she'd tell Harland. 'But the prognosis is good.'

It was strange, then, when he finally showed up two weeks later with a gash across his forehead. For a moment Marie was confused, as if Harland's injury were somehow connected to the chair. The boy's cut was crudely mended with tiny adhesive bandages.

'Are you okay?'

'What?' he said – and when she pointed to his head, he told her it was nothing, it was old.

'You didn't have it the last time I saw you.'

'Maybe you didn't notice.'

'I would have noticed.'

Harland rolled his eyes – and when Marie asked him what did *that* mean, he said, 'Nothing. You were just a little . . .'

'A little what?'

'Listen, why don't you just tell me what you want me to do today – cause I won't have a lot of time now that school's starting up.'

'Is it September already? I had no idea. I need to get a calculator. I mean a – what do you call it? For the dates?'

Harland looked down.

Marie took a step back, in case he could smell her breath. 'Well, maybe you should do a little pickup outside and then . . .' She glanced out the window, looking for her train of thought. 'You know, I still want you to come by when you have school. I can help you.'

'Help me with what?'

'I don't know. English.'

'I'm past help,' said Harland. 'I failed like three things last year.' He squinted toward the hills. 'I better go get started out there.'

'Why bother? Just come in and have something to eat.'

'Nah. If I don't do any work –'

'Don't worry,' slurred Marie. 'I'll pay you anyway.'

'For what?'

'Well, we'll have to negotiate. Maybe you can read to me.'

'Are you *kidding*?' said Harland.

'Do I look like I'm kidding?'

'You look like you need to sit down.' He took her arm and led her to the couch.

The monsoons came late that year, and when they did, it was biblical. The skies cracked with demonic wrath, and the rain hissed when it touched the earth. The soaked hills gurgled and steamed. Frantic birds darted in search of blue, while the cows and chickens fled for the ark of higher ground, which was near the McGregors' house. Marie's cottage developed a moat, and when it finally dried, the shape of the land had changed. There were furrows that seemed perfect for planting a garden. Marie put in some collards and kale, tossed a few packets of wildflower seeds – lupine and bluebells. She cut away the carelessweed that had come up beside the porch.

The weather was finally cooler. When Harland came over now, he was usually dressed in a flannel shirt. Sometimes he matched his plaid chair perfectly. The cut on his head had healed, and though other bruises appeared now and then, he never offered explanations, and Marie didn't pry. She simply let him know that he was welcome to visit whenever he liked.

Despite the open invitation, he came only once a week. Occasionally he didn't show, which set Marie on edge. It took some effort to keep herself from knocking on the McGregors' door. She'd started to worry about the kid. When he did visit, it was always a Tuesday (Marie had a calendar now), and always after school.

They were still on part one of *Anna Karenina*. Harland had tried to squirm out of it at first, but Marie had insisted. 'Reading it will improve you.'

'Do I need improvement?'

'I hate to tell you this, Harland, but we all do. It's our life's work.'

Sometimes, when she said things like this, he took away her lemonade and poured her a glass of milk.

'I just don't understand why I have to read it out loud.'

'That way, you'll never forget. The words will stick.'

For a while he remained unconvinced, stopping often to comment. After the very first sentence, he'd said, 'Well I coulda told you that.'

'Shut up and read,' she'd commanded.

'Why are the letters so big, though?'

'The better to see you with, my dear,' she told him – though she was pretty sure this made no sense. 'Come on.' She snapped her fingers. 'Read.'

'Everything was in con-fu – confusion – in the O-blon-skys' house…'

Marie often closed her eyes to listen to his nervous, halting voice – a harsh fiddle playing a waltz. She could picture him swaying on a tightrope, crossing the abyss of all he didn't know. Of course, the person up there in danger might have been her. She'd gotten so used to her loneliness, she didn't want to fall from it now. Sometimes she corrected Harland's pronunciation or explained a word he was unfamiliar with. *Calumny, epaulet, samovar.*

Marie made him read for at least half an hour. He didn't get dessert until he was done. While they ate, they talked a bit, but never about important things. They talked about the weather or school, about movies or places they'd like to visit. Their conversations, after Tolstoy, were nothing much to record – but their silences, Marie felt, were literary. Harland, like her, was a great starer, and they often looked at the wall as if there were a window in it.

When he went home, she often felt sad. She knew she was probably confusing things, thinking about something old, something that had nothing to do with the boy, but she chose not to examine this too deeply. Why tarnish with psychology something so simple and pure? A pureness perhaps slightly muddied already by the fact that she continued to give the boy, at the end of every visit, a hundred-dollar bill.

After he was gone, she often switched from milk to gin, though she never poured herself as much as she would have before. When she woke in the mornings now, it was not so much with a headache as with a dull sorrow that felt like an improvement.

They were dead. They would always be dead. So what if they hadn't been the most loving parents. Whatever unfinished business she had with them had to be settled here, among the living.

One morning, she even had the bravery to go to the suitcase of relics and take out the small Higgins she'd kept. The frame was long gone, and the canvas was wrapped tightly with two summer dresses and a madman's worth of twine. She released it from its swaddling and hung it in the living room, near the La-Z-Boy.

It was different from the ones she'd sold. This one was a simple painting of hills, very modest, almost abstract. It didn't attempt to tell a story. It was all about the light. Less a place than a feeling.

Harland, she hoped, would like it.

T he next week, of course, he didn't come. But on a Wednesday morning Mrs McGregor did. She was dressed in a thuggish raincoat and bore no eggs. The small talk (*good morning, how are you, that rain!*) lasted all of thirty seconds before the woman got to it.

'I'm really not sure what's going on over here, but I sure as hell hope we won't need to call the police.'

'The police?' said Marie. 'Why would you call the police?'

'You tell me,' said Mrs McGregor.

Marie asked the woman if she'd like to come inside.

'What I'd *like* is to know what you and Harland are up to.'

'We're just – please, why don't you come inside?'

When Mrs McGregor stepped warily into the cottage, Marie gestured toward the books. 'Harland and I have been doing some reading.'

'Doing what?'

Marie realized how ridiculous this sounded, so she added: 'Plus, we eat. You know, he has a big appetite, and it turns out I'm quite a good baker. I actually just made strudel.'

'Are you drunk?' asked Mrs McGregor. 'Cause I seen the bottles.'

And I see where Harland picked up his lovely grammar, Marie wanted to say. Instead, she apologized.

'And what is *this*?' The woman pulled the hundreds from her pocket – snapped the fan of bills like a flamenco dancer.

'It's just a tip. A gift. He does some work outside and –'

'This is a pretty big tip for picking up cow shit.'

'Well, he does other things. I mean, he . . . honestly, there's nothing unwholesome going on.'

'And where do you get this kind of money, no job or nothing? Because if there's anything illegal happening over here –'

'There's not. I swear.'

Mrs McGregor snorted. 'Don't matter anyway, cause your six months is up.'

'Yes,' said Marie. 'I realize that. I was actually going to suggest paying another six in advance.'

'No. You keep your money.'

'I can pay you right now,' said Marie. 'In cash.'

Mrs McGregor suddenly looked exhausted. 'What are you even doing here, person like you?'

'I'm – I like it here. If you want, I'd be willing to pay a full year upfront.'

'Why would you do that? See now, that just makes me think there's something seriously wrong with you, lady.'

'Please,' said Marie. 'I'd really like to stay. Harland and I are just friends.'

'The boy is fifteen.'

'Well, what does that mean? You and I are probably around the same age. Aren't *you* friends with him?'

'No I'm not *friends* with him. He's my fucking son. We'll give you a week to get yourself packed.'

Marie started to shake. 'Okay, just let me – can we just talk about this?'

'No, we can't,' said Mrs McGregor.

Outside the open door, rain began to fall. The smell of creosote flooded the house. Marie crossed the room and sunk into Harland's chair. She looked at the Higgins – the hazy hills, the blurred light. When she stood again, she was shaking even more.

'You evict me and I'll report you.'

'Report me?'

'Yes. You and your husband.'

'For *what?*'

'As I said, Harland and I are friends.'

'And what does he tell you? Cause he's a liar, too.'

'How's the little girl?' asked Marie. 'How's her ankle?'

The woman's face turned a stunning shade of red.

'Do you think I can't hear you over there?' continued Marie.

When Mrs McGregor clenched her fists, Marie backed away.

The woman didn't move, though. Her eyes filled with tears. 'That's not your business.'

As they looked at each other, Marie could feel her own shame push against Mrs McGregor's, the force as real, as implacable, as opposing magnets.

It seemed a defiance of some physical law when Marie found herself touching the woman's arm.

'Please. I'm not doing anything to harm your son.'

'You better not be, lady.' Mrs McGregor pulled her arm away. 'Cause he's got enough of that already.'

In the silence that followed, a cow lowed. Both women looked at the floor.

'He's safe over here,' said Marie.

'So you say.' Mrs McGregor kept her eyes down. 'If we didn't need the cash, you'd be out on your ass.'

'I can drop it by tomorrow,' said Marie.

'Rent'll probably be going up.'

'That's fine.'

'Probably a hundred more a month.'

'Perfectly reasonable.'

The woman made a terrible sound, a defeated laugh, then put Harland's money in her pocket.

After she left, Marie couldn't breathe. And when she could, there was still the stench of creosote. She'd known that smell her whole life, had probably first smelled it from inside her mother's womb. It was the scent of Tucson – tarry, dank, a bitter cloy of chocolate. Once, as a child, she'd collected the leaves and tried to smoke them like the

Indians used to. She was always doing crazy things, running around with boys. Her father had called her a desert rat. Her mother had called her disgusting, picking cactus spines from her arms and cholla stems from her clothing. Pushing her away after she'd groomed her: 'Go to your room now. I can't stand to look at you.'

The day after she'd delivered the money – a fat envelope of cash – Marie noticed Mr McGregor lurking around the hills, closer to the cottage than she'd ever seen him before. The next evening he was there, too. Marie stayed inside and tried to read, but it was no use – she couldn't concentrate. Was he trying to intimidate her? She locked the door and waited for Harland.

But the boy didn't come.

Marie wondered if she should pack. Run off during the night.

She hadn't done anything wrong, though. She decided to stand her ground.

Why had she thought these people were Christians? She tried to recall her first conversations with them, and suspected that what she'd seen as politeness was actually fear. Marie had shown up, that first day, dressed in Miu Miu slacks and a Burberry trench coat. The McGregors had been wearing the sartorial equivalent of mud flaps. Their big house was falling apart. They were clearly struggling, and desperate for a tenant. A tenant who wouldn't mind the animals, or that the property turned into a cesspool whenever it rained.

Maybe Mr McGregor was planning to break into the cottage and rob her.

Do it, she thought. Take everything. What did it matter? For years, actually, she'd been hoping someone might relieve her of her burden. Though she kept some money in the bank, most of it was in the suitcase.

Marie liked the risk of it, the ease. Liked how it kept the dead from sleeping. How it kept them anxious, and therefore present.

Her parents had never been generous. As a child, they'd given her food and shelter, but never any money. And though they'd paid her college tuition, Marie had had to work two jobs to cover living expenses.

It was some kind of lesson, she supposed – possibly a good one. She'd become a capable girl. And the truth was: she'd never really minded that her parents were selfish, spending most of their money feathering their nest, their fortress in the Rincons. Still, it had been sad to watch them become nervous prisoners. After retiring, her father had grown paranoid. He'd had elaborate alarm systems installed on the property. He'd even taken down the paintings and locked them in a vault.

It had been Marie who suggested her parents take a trip. With her meager earnings from the gallery, she'd even paid for the lodge near Canyon de Chelly, as well as sent them a gift card for the gas.

Sometimes, under the spell of gin, she imagined they were grateful. She'd helped them escape, hadn't she? That house of privilege and padlocks, the old dog crapping under tables – it was nothing short of hell.

When Harland finally showed up a few weeks later, Marie was in a state. He knocked, as he'd done the first time, on the bedroom window.

'Come around the front,' she told him – but he said no, he didn't want anyone to see him.

Marie's heart was racing as the boy climbed through the window. She quickly led him from the bedroom into the living area.

'It's after midnight, Harland.'

'I'm sorry, Marie.'

It was the first time he'd ever said her name. 'Is everything okay?' she asked. 'Are you in danger?'

He told her he was just having a bad night, he couldn't sleep. 'I thought maybe we could read or something.'

'Do your parents know you're here?'

'No. They're in bed.'

'I'm sure your mother told you not to visit me.'

'She didn't tell me shit. She took my money, though.'

'I'm sorry.'

'I don't care. They need it more than I do.'

Marie, feeling dizzy, sat down, while Harland went into the kitchen and poured out two glasses of milk. 'I'll bring you some of the good stuff,' he said. 'From the cows. If you want it.'

'What about your sister?'

'What about her?'

'I'm worried about her.'

'Why?'

'Your father.'

Harland's face turned bright red – obviously a McGregor trait. 'My father?'

'I thought Lacy's ankle was –'

'No fucking way,' said Harland. 'That happened at school. No way! If he ever pulled that shit on her, I'd fucking kill him.'

'Don't say things like that. I'm worried about you, too.'

'Nah. I'll be fine. Anyway, now that he's got some money, he'll be calmer. Can we not talk anymore and just read?'

'Harland, I don't know if you should be here.'

'You want me to leave?'

He looked at her in a way she couldn't bear. She turned on the lamp and handed him volume one. They were only about a hundred pages in. Nineteen hundred more to go.

'Shit,' said Harland. 'We might be doing this forever.'

'It does have an ending,' said Marie.

'A good one?'

She tried to smile. 'You'll have to give me your opinion when we get there.'

S ometimes he came three days in a row, but then there were long stretches when he stopped by only once a month, or less.

'I'm here for the shit,' he'd often say when he arrived – which now meant Tolstoy. Harland wasn't a fan; he didn't care for Anna. 'She's a horrible person, don't you think?' he said one day.

When Marie shrugged, Harland said, 'What's wrong?'

'Nothing.'

'What? Is she like your favorite person in the world or something?'

'No. But I don't dislike her as much as you do.'

'She's just so selfish.'

'Well, I don't think Tolstoy liked her either.'

'Who's that?'

'The *author*?' said Marie.

'Oh, right. That's pretty weird, though. I mean, how do you write two thousand pages about someone you don't like? Then name the book after her.' Harland spooned up some pudding. 'So, is she, like, gonna marry that Vronsky guy?'

'I'm not telling you.'

So they kept reading – Harland always in his chair, and Marie on the couch. Some afternoons, there were fresh bruises. Usually, Marie made no comment, though sometimes she couldn't help herself: 'You will escape one day. You know that, right?'

It was Harland's turn to shrug.

'You will.' Marie liked telling him this, and it seemed that he liked hearing it.

Page by page, it progressed. Kitty fell ill, Anna got pregnant, Vronsky attempted suicide.

Every summer, the rains came and went. The yard flooded; the garden thrived.

Eventually, Harland started combing his hair differently – and when he was seventeen he grew it long, though Marie never got close enough to tell if it smelled like bubblegum. Sometimes he told her about his girlfriends, or a road trip he was taking with some buddies. Harland was driving now. Marie let him use the Volvo.

Sometimes, as he read, she sketched him. 'Don't roll your eyes.'

Whenever she offered money, he mostly refused it, but now and then he accepted it gravely with a nod: 'Probably I'll just give it to *them*.'

'That reminds me. I have some milk bottles for you to bring back to your mother. Don't forget to take them.'

'Do you need more eggs?'

'I'm good right now.'

When Harland got into college, Marie felt an almost painful pride. She'd helped him with his applications. He'd been accepted at two schools – neither great, both out-of-state. Harland chose New Mexico.

The day he left, Marie held back her tears, so as not to compete with Mrs McGregor. At the cottage, she offered him the final two volumes of Tolstoy – but Harland said, 'No. We'll finish it when I get back.'

Marie didn't argue. She gave him some money instead.

Outside, behind the carelessweed, Harland leaned in as if to kiss her, but Marie only smirked and told him not to be dramatic.

He met a girl, of course. After college, he moved to Ohio. Whenever he visited Tucson, he always stopped by.

'I miss talking to you, Marie.'

She told him he could call her anytime.

But he never did.

For a while, Marie dated again – a man named Thomas, who cleaned out air ducts. 'You wouldn't believe what gets up in there,' he told her. She said she didn't want to know. He was funny; he liked to drink. They had a fair amount of fun. She didn't read much anymore, but she kept the books on her shelves. Occasionally she took one down and picked out a sentence – speaking it out loud, then swallowing it like a vitamin.

There were a few rough years, to be honest. *Hairy*, Harland would have called them. And it was true. Time was a beast, a hairy little fucker. Marie thinned out the loneliness with gin. She was well into her fifties now.

Twice a year she had dinner with the family. When she got sick, it was Mrs McGregor who took her to the hospital. The air-duct man was long gone. Marie got better, came home – but then, several years later, she collapsed one morning in the yard, a terrible pain in her gut.

'I did this to myself,' she said, but Linda (Mrs McGregor) said, 'Don't talk like that.'

At first, she thought it was a boy she'd known in high school – but the hair was the wrong color; the skin, too.

'You didn't have to come,' she said.

Harland just tilted his head: *don't be silly.*

'Did you fly here?' she asked him. 'From . . .'

'Ohio,' he reminded her.

'I used to know a song about Ohio, but I can't remember it.'

He sat beside the hospital bed and took her hand. 'It's bad, right? Mom says it's . . .'

'It's not good.' She handed him a magazine, something the nurse had left in the room.

'What's this for?'

'I don't have anything better. All my books are at the house.'

So, he read her an article about camping in the Apennines – but only made it through a few paragraphs before he stopped.

'Sweet boy, don't cry.' And then she told him, 'Go ahead, let it out,' because clearly he couldn't stop and she didn't want him to feel ashamed for it.

It washed over her and she felt clean.

As he dried his eyes, he laughed. 'The nurse asked if you were my mother.'

'What'd you tell her?'

'I told her, yes.'

Marie nodded.

'But I never really thought of you that way,' he continued.

She patted his hand, said she was very glad to hear it.

He didn't come again, or if he did, she didn't see him. She dreamed all the time now. The pain was gone. Often in her dreams she was drunk.

When she floated back to the small white room, there were sometimes guests: Linda and Lacy – even that Thomas fellow came by to visit. She never stayed with them long, though. She wanted to get back to her drunken dreams. Morphine was something else.

Marie wished that her parents had not gone so quickly; that they, too, could have had something like this. This dream of life, as you lay dying. It was more than she'd thought – her sixty-something years. Fascinating how quickly the mundane faded, and all that was left were the brilliant patches of color.

The small Higgins was left to Harland, as well as most of the money. Linda and Lacy were not neglected.

'She was a crazy fucking lady.'

Harland told his sister to shut up.

'Why are you keeping that piece of crap?' she asked as he lugged the La-Z-Boy into the back of his pickup.

He offered no explanation.

He spent a day going though her things – packed up most of the clothes and relics in a box for St Vincent de Paul. He debated over *Anna K*, and decided to leave her for the next tenant. He was pretty sure he knew how it ended. He left the recipe cards, too. His wife was a terrible cook and fussy about her weight.

As for the drawings, he took all he could find, though he didn't look at them until he got back to Ohio. And then he sat on his chair and went through them. Again and again, his face as a teenager – sometimes sullen, sometimes bruised, sometimes squinting like a pirate.

Harland shook his head, amazed that she'd somehow done it – improved him. Hell, she'd nearly made him beautiful. ∎

Serpent lady, 2009

DIARIES

Suzanne Brøgger

TRANSLATED FROM THE DANISH BY THE AUTHOR

Knudstrup School, Løve
29 May 1985

ANNOUNCEMENT
For many years a certain individual has been sending letters to people in
Denmark, and abroad, in the name of Suzanne Brøgger. In order to avoid
further confusion, we are obliged in this untraditional way to bring attention
to the situation in the hope of stopping the unwanted epistolary activity.
Rhodos,
The Publisher

This is the best thing that has ever been written in the news about
me, or rather, concerning me. (Nobody has ever written about me.)
By now the press has gone wild and my publisher is protecting me
by saying that I'm in France. Journalists are asking why we haven't
reported this character to the police? *But how can you have an officer
sitting at her desk while she is at her task pretending she is me?* People
want to know what she is writing in my name, they demand quotes
from her letters to Régis Debray, Jack Lang, the French Minister of
Culture, the Mexican ambassador, etc., and they want to know *who*
she is. My publisher won't reveal her name though, because she may

sue, and even though she would lose, it is depressing for me to spend more time on her. In fact: if only she would take over – not me – but my public functions, that would be great. Then the media would discover her identity, get interested in *her*, and she would use her talent acting as 'me', and get credit for her brilliant intelligence. That way she would get so much satisfaction out of being Lizette that she would hopefully lose interest in me. But as Z, my new beloved, so pointedly remarks: She would get the attention of a loony! And that would kill her!

I hadn't thought of that.

2 June 1985

I'm trying to write my lecture for the Finland Lit Festival, like a good student. The unity between thought and action, dream & reality in my life has been too claustrophobic. The consequences of 'I live as I write and I write as I live' – devastating. I almost died. For truth alone. Dangerous idealism, dying as a witness. As in the Nazi camps, where idea and action came together with no room for the symbolic. And like the stalker Frode who terrorises me, on a daily basis, throwing pebbles at my window at night. In our hyperrealistic world we have lost the sense of the symbolic.

Z and I paint the house and make love. Yesterday he mended the chainsaw, the hedges fell and a new landscape emerged. I'm like the sleeping so-so-beauty who has woken up.

Only, I miss dreaming.

7 June 1985

Today I can dream, because he is not here, so now I miss him. My habit of being a dreamer is filled with the joy of melancholy. Nevertheless the thrill of nightly ecstasy makes me meek. Never in my life have I felt such deep bliss – every night even! If only we don't wear each other out!

I shall not let any past experience interfere with the future.

8 June 1985

Shocking article: '*La falsification et le consensus*' – if you pay one cent more than required you may hurt the 'system' or drive it insane. Whereas any number of 'red brigades' – incurable romantics, as they believe that the state has a heart which may be wounded – cannot hurt a fly. OK, a fly. Someone sent a fake poem by Pasolini. But what if this becomes the norm, faking it?

Like the Gestapo times, at the end of the war, when nobody could trust each other and consensus was dissolved, '*la guerre de tous contre tous*'. Then not only power relations are destroyed but the precondition for survival of the group *tout court*.

A day of dreaming. I'm not conscious of what I'm doing, since I have never before in my life lived with anyone. But Z has registered this state of dreaming in which I live, connecting it with the power of my writing, the fact that I hardly ever rewrite or correct anything. Most of it happens in this fugue-like state, this life in slow motion, which is just as important to me as sleep is for others. Still – and this is crucial for me – I don't seem absent-minded when I speak with him.

Tomorrow, singing games in the garden. Z will be elsewhere attending some student jubilee.

Rain and stormy weather – but we pulled it off, the fourteen of us, Rigmor with her silver hip replacement, high as a lark. Tarab Tulku gave me an ancient Tibetan gold ring as a gift. Z came when everybody was leaving. Because I'm in love I was not totally *there*. Now, back to everyday life, the best.

11 June 1985

In Z's opinion we ought to buy a washing machine. Because every time I go to the neighbours with my laundry basket asking for a favour, he thinks I give them power over me. He doesn't know the secret of country life: interdependency. But he's probably right. Not only in relation to my neighbours but to everybody. I tend to empower people. Because instinctively I see them as weak. Maybe I'm wrong.

12 June 1985

I am writing about the exhibition in Paris, *Les Immatériaux*, for the radio. (Bewildered as to whether I should show Z what I'm working on? Basically I'm a terribly private person.) He hasn't slept a wink, the poor dear, the retrospective horror of having stayed too long in his marriage, shipwrecked friendships, betrayal and joy keeps him awake. I woke up, drenched in tears, dreaming that I had to be with my sister.
  Rain all day long.

14 June 1985

Home. The nightmares of Z. No wonder. The change of life. You have to make room for that. His parents died upstairs in his childhood villa. He could only see his mother through the window of a tent. First his father died when Z was one year old. Then his mother when he was two. (Parents met and fell in love in a tuberculosis sanatorium.) The man who is my beloved is grounded in death and loss. Where you would expect something there was nothing. The *ungivenness* of things. My love is the passion fruit of death. What will this bring – something instead of nothing?

15 June 1985

Z has gone to Lolland to fetch his daughter while I'm labouring to complete my Finnish speech. I have been living by myself all my life – and now I find it hard to spend one day without him! He has written to stalker F that the reason I have not reported him to the police –

which he so desperately wants me to – is that I don't read his mail. It is now being taken care of by my mate. Bye-bye F. I pray that from now on the stranger F will leave me alone.

17 June 1985

Played with Claes Andersson, the Finnish poet & pianist. Dreading the literary festival in Lahti. I have prepared my speech, but this seems more like a three-day booze party with big bad wolves – or rather drunken wolves. How to avoid . . . Must I expose myself to social activities? Have to share a room for three days, this is very difficult for me. I'm writing under a neon light while the others are dancing with their name tags on – fifties pop. I ended up at a horrible table with two Finnish journalists. Then came Claude Simon. But he is – like many writers – so self-absorbed, difficult to talk to, he probably just wants to go back to his vineyard where he lives as a peasant. Özdemir wants to translate my novel into Turkish. A devoted reader from Lapland wanted to stage *Tone* near the Arctic Circle. So this is what literary festivals are for. Danced with an *obsédé*, subjected myself to an obnoxious lecture about gays, that they 'do it in the exhaust pipe'. He ranted on about a Danish writer who had been raped in Uzbekistan, whether I knew her?

Did I know her!

18 June 1985

At such a male conference I become an ardent feminist. The all-women evening in the sauna by the lake where we beat ourselves with fresh birch branches and covered our faces with leaves from the smoke – what a relief! Quite medieval this sight of full-fleshed female nudes on the background of black wood. Nymphs and witches with sod on their bottoms and smoke on their backs came swishing, steaming, into the lake. Wonderfully exhausted we lit a huge fire and chatted. *The Kalevala* was quoted, lamentations and poems were recited and sung and, all excited, we were asking: what happens next? The storyteller had a PhD in *The Kalevala* but she told the story in the oral tradition of the feminine mode in starts and jumps oblivious to linear cause & effect. A pottery maker said that her father was a famous Finnish scholar of Kierkegaard. And an interpreter who had been a great soprano said that a year ago she lost her voice. But the most interesting thing, maybe, was hearing about the forgotten tradition of *lamenteuses*, women who in rites of loss and separation perform their tearful poems and songs. If I can't be a writer, I want to be a professional mourner. Weeping willow, lovely evening.

20 June 1985

So I became a *feminist* for four days! I was elected to sit on a phallic panel for the finals – a form that I really detest. A prison of words, all those inflated, mono-mono-monologues.

Without knowing it I made a blunder: it turns out that the story of the two kinds of laughter, the one of the angels and the one of the devil, comes from a novel by Kundera that I haven't read. Most probably I may have read something in the *New Yorker* long ago when I didn't know this Czech author. I must have absorbed the story as a myth, ancient knowledge (which it probably is). Some Finnish newspaper made a scandal of my ignorance. Rightly so. And strangely so. Because all those people whose language comes from Marxism, Structuralism, Derrida or Foucault, or the implicitly unsaid on which they build their narratives & concept of life – that is allowed, accepted, even the rule. Very rarely do people put themselves at stake, speak on their own.

A man named Kari follows faithfully in my footsteps. People call him my bodyguard. It turns out that he is a communist and comes from the most red town in Finland, called Kemi.

Wonderful sailing trip with song and harmonica. Tomorrow – home. Discharge.

21 June 1985

Halldór Laxness: '*It is my own firm belief that you mustn't kill more people than you yourself can eat.*'

Happiness, happiness, home – and with my love at last.

Woe is me! Frode my stalker has been here. It makes me sick. It hurts all over; I have the suicidal pain of giving up. The struggle has exhausted me, although it does help that Z is here and that he has talked to F. Only this has infuriated F and he has reported the incident to the police claiming that I am being held prisoner in my own home, denied my freedom. The police called to check whether it was true! F wants to go to court. He is threatening to come back in order to get arrested. He has repeatedly called the police to report his own transgression: 'Now I have disobeyed the police's orders again – aren't you going to do something about it?'

Will do. Tomorrow I shall have to collect information about dates and time for the police. *Ça m'emmerde.* But Z is a healing bandage on the wound. He has an appointment with a lawyer to get a quick divorce. The dog is a problem – among many others – partly because he may have to put it to sleep.

He is painting his room, and has brought along his own pictures. Also he has mown the lawn. Also there was another letter from Lizette. Z is probably right in suggesting that it is I who will have to change my attitude towards the loonies. Because they will always be there. One or the other.

We have eaten pheasant and rhubarb pie in celebration of the four years since Z got his doctorate, and the Brandes Prize, and mentioned me in his thank-you speech, which is when our minds began to cross-fertilise. And now it's four months since our bodies did the same. In the course of four months our lives have completely changed.

23 June 1985

Last night, at three in the morning, my stalker came. Z woke up hearing yelling and banging on the door, the ringing of the bell. We armed ourselves with kitchen knives and scissors. I took my ivory letter opener. We called the police; the stalker was insane, and they arrested him. The next morning we had to drive to the police station and report. I could document thirteen transgressions of the police order since 4 December. But the officer had already decided before hearing my case – that the stalker should be released. Frode refused to respond to the police, saying that he would only speak in court. (Conceited?) He wants to get arrested in order to speak in court! A thorn in the flesh. Z is overwhelmed by the beastliness I've had to endure alone for all these years. He himself is ready to murder although he also feels pity for the pathetic perpetrator.

Today, out of the blue, Z had an attack of jealousy – a lifelong affliction of his. As long as it doesn't interfere with me!

Carmen McRae: '*Here again is that prime rule: SING. Sing all the time. Sing with the radio, with records, with the canned music in grocery stores and elevators. Sing with the piano ... Sing without accompaniment. Sing all the time.*'

24 June 1985

I am bestowed the deepest joy as though my whole life had just been a preparation for being with Z. Whether we trim or cut the hedges, talk about Plato or make love – when he lies down beside me miracles happen – and daily. I have never experienced this in my whole life, but when I tell friends & others about my new relationship – or my new life really – people just say: 'Great!' No adequate reactions. Which means that it is not through this binding love that I communicate to the external world. This has now become my 'private life' – a sphere I never knew before.

Ole is in the hospital afflicted with side effects of Aids – tuberculosis of the intestines and surgery for appendicitis. He has given up his studio in New York.

25 June 1985

Today Z has painted or rather stroked my windowpanes with a white 'sugar' coating; I'll eat them in my dreams. At the same time there has been turbulence in the house what with the new fridge, the infernal noise of the man with the sander competing with the sounds of the piano tuner.

Z's room now looks like an artist's studio in white rather than the small, old-fashioned, green drawing room that I decorated. He tells me horror stories from his marriage, with himself in the part of monster number one. I'm listening like an anthropologist to these exotic manners, as if I'll never be part of this. It's a classic: he is looking in me for what he crushed in his former wife. But my history is different. I no longer fear the risk of being destroyed by another human being. I can only be fulfilled, like a rebirth, integration & synthesis with a man. This is my project now: to integrate a man in the material (me) that I have already embraced, oxidised and worked through the mixer. (Love affairs.) Hélène Cixous wrote that the woman who had been through murder and rape could only survive by getting a new body so that death and violence would retreat to a symbolic space. I have tried to turn everything into reality. In the end there was only my own death left to materialise. But now I'm about to internalise the man in my own reality, which is – admittedly – an attachment. But hopefully also the establishment of a symbolic space for creation.

28 June 1985

The dentist can't operate or give me antibiotics in case I'm pregnant – which is probably not within reach at my age and not even my goal

– but on the other hand I'm too old to prevent it actively. I'll just let life decide. 'Life' has always been my best adviser whereas me . . . I've always been good at making the wrong decisions.

29 June 1985

Another fan letter today of the more sinister kind, from a Norwegian woman who writes about the man she loved – and whom everybody loved. He is the one who wrote to me, saying that he would fly down to Denmark to eat fried plaice with me before he died. The doctors hadn't given him long to live. I never answered. One can't eat fried plaice with all the people who have to die.

Now the girlfriend/secretary sends me the stranger's obituary plus a letter he wrote for me just before his exit: 'When you read this letter, I'll already be down yonder.' He regrets not having had his last wish fulfilled and reckons after having read *Crème Fraiche* that I misunderstood him, suspecting that he wanted to take me to bed, but that he was impotent due to his illness. Again he writes about the shape of my lips, concluding that I don't know what love is. Had I eaten fried plaice with him, he might have assumed something else.

It feels depressing to receive a letter from the dead. People write to a 'symbol' – not realising that they are actually addressing a human being who is baking a rhubarb pie and cutting her roses.

In the middle of the night Frode turned up, so scary, and again this afternoon Z talked to him for twenty minutes explaining that if his love for me was so great, the best way to show it would be to leave me in peace. F wants to hear a 'no' from my own lips, but how could I ever convince him that it is my own 'no' since he considers me imprisoned, deprived of my freedom!

The feeling of hopelessness is still there, but since Z is here as well I'm not bothered in the same way as before. I don't feel that it is killing me any more; that my life is threatened.

1 July 1985

Today Frode was here again. I came to the door yelling NO. 'No to what?' he said quietly, wanting to discuss it. I called the police, for the third time that day. I wrote a small text for a magazine, Z suggested cuts. I accept his advice, *pourquoi pas?*

In town I visited Ole at the hospital. He is already an old man with Aids, cancer, tuberculosis and an infected appendicitis wound that won't heal. 'Thank you for everything,' he said. He is still making plans, but part of his being is already turned away towards the beyond. Since he had to give up his studio in New York he is obsessed with the here and now, hospital routines, a button that doesn't work, the meaning of a light signal . . . He is lying there with an open stomach having had the stitches removed because of an infection, only this black hole with a light piece of gauze over it.

Fleur attended a wedding in New York where the septic tank leaked and the guests slipped in shit from the lavatories. The wedding couldn't get started because a funeral was still on, with musicians playing off-key. This was the revenge, as Fleur said, because the bride wouldn't invite her sisters' boyfriends as they – according to the bride – were all living in sin. The bride only wanted silverware, twenty-four of each, instead of which she got death and shit.

Days of plenty are rushing by, I still get my work done in the morning. I may have to write a lecture for the Danish Academy in Rome – I may write about 'Influences & Inspirations', which I could also use for my second *Brøg* anthology.

Z is reading Sophus Claussen. He wants to write his biography in his new white room, with his friend Kurt Trampedach on the wall as well as *The Lady and the Unicorn*, our trademark. *À mon seul désir*, the dedication he wanted from me in my book about the lady.

We are overjoyed & exhausted from lovemaking, he is sweet and gentle in all respects and has completely entered my life.

8 July 1985

Glazed rose petals for dessert. Recipe: in the evening you pick fresh rose petals and place them carefully on a piece of linen. Break an egg and throw away the yolk. With a mink brush paint each petal carefully with the egg white and dip it in sugar with the help of tweezers. Put to dry on parchment paper in rays from the sun on a quiet day with no wind!

Today a friend of Z came over to get feedback on his doctorate about Utopia. Z told him to rewrite the whole thing. The friend left rather nonplussed.

In the morning the police came.

9 July 1985

Three crazy people in one day. The one who sends me presents every day and signs his name: Georg Brandes. He admits to being obsessed with me, I never answer.

Frode came. We didn't open the door, and immediately called the police. Luckily he fell into a discussion with the neighbours so he was still around when the police came to get him. Z sleeps every night with a bread knife.

New York, New York with De Niro as a psychopath. Don't need movies.

Got around to calling Erling who was pleased that I had not excluded him entirely from my new life. Finally he admits to being enthusiastic about Judith's book. He has never known the depths of Karen's life – he called her Karen – so when she actually telephoned him once in the middle of the night shouting: 'Do you love me?', he decided to send her a fresh rose every day. They never talked about it, and she never thanked him. But they knew. And she knew that Erling dreaded depths. Once he lost his lover in the waves of the Danube.

Reading Spinoza.

Z calls the people in our region the 'gastronauts'. They sacrifice food to their one and only god: the mighty belly. Their only function in life is to carry their huge paunches, boosting their bellies to make sure they are always fully distended.

11 July 1985

Z suggests that the only way the crazy people may be pacified is if I institutionalise myself and marry him.

Next week the stalker court case. What really worries me is that it will be about whether I really mean it, the police order! Whether I'm serious about it! What? This is what makes me lose my will to live. They also ask whether I insist on having the trial behind closed doors, otherwise it would be hard to keep away the tabloids. At first I thought that it would be in my interest to have Frode exposed, making a fool out of him. But then it turns out that *I* would be the fool – which is proof of the failure of my life – i.e. this case is really to the advantage of F! The public prosecutor calls the whole thing 'a seedy side effect of expedient marketing'. Obviously they know what marketing is, I don't. I have only written my books and after that – been pestered.

Yes, I'm ready to marry Z, but first he must get a divorce, let's abide by the law.

12 July 1985

My friends hope that the trial won't make me emigrate. Could it really turn out to be to the defendant's advantage if they interrogate me on whether I really 'mean it', the police order! Kafkaesque! Why don't I want to be a cockroach? Explain! But why am I at a loss when it comes to explaining why I don't want to see my stalker? Z comforts me by saying that one sentence only will be necessary: 'The public is not admitted on my private territory.'

I once wrote an essay titled 'Let's Give Up Private Life'. I have spent the rest of my life reclaiming it.

15 July 1985

Z has been in hell because of his furious ex-wife who wants to destroy him. But now he'll get a lawyer of his own. He has given me an ancient silver coin, Demeter, the goddess of fertility and growth. My beloved. Wasn't Demeter seduced by Pluto and then sent into Hades, while her mother Persephone had it arranged so that Demeter only had to spend half of the year underground and half of the year on Earth? And that's how we got the seasons, sowing and harvest.

Z has painted the car against rust; I have ironed curtains and written the second version of *Gay Death.*

Rupert Sheldrake's work on how forms appear: '*Form isn't a conserved quantity – if you burn a rose to ashes, the mass and energy are conserved, but the form of the flower is simply destroyed.*'

17 July 1985

Annoying day. Frode didn't show up in court, and they couldn't interrogate me, a work day wasted. I have to wait for another call. Luckily Z is with me, although he seems somewhat depressed these days. His upcoming divorce maybe? His insomnia? He is a tense, nervous workaholic. But as long as he doesn't blame me for his moods, I guess I can live with it. Obviously it is not common to be a joybird like me, singing all day long. Aren't we all characterised by the sort of challenges we have because they reveal *who* we are?

Madame de Staël: '*La gloire est que le deuil éclatant du bonheur.*'

21 July 1985

Yesterday it was five months since Z came here for the first time. But I live with him beyond time and space; he has only been here one second, everything is new and yet he has been here always. But I can't write about him, maybe because I don't want to. I don't want to make him into literature, I want to make him into my life. I am a couple of days late in my cycle . . . Is that because of Demeter's coin that he placed under my pillow? I bought a good pair of scissors so that I can cut his hair without him looking like Vespasian or a monk. Last night I cooked avocado soup and *les poires au vin* with vanilla sauce!

One morning I woke up weeping with the thought that he didn't love me and wasn't happy here with me. But this was ancient anxiety from the past having nothing to do with the present.

Reread *L'hypothèse d'Eros* for my essay on sources of inspiration. Wonder why it once excited me so.

I'm living in an ecstatic cloud of happiness that I cannot fathom in writing. I only know that I'm no longer an astral body, but earthbound. This is what Z activates in me: earth, laughter and appetite.

I bring the song.

23 July 1985

My period is five days late. Feel feverish, shivering, swollen, sore breasts, dizzy when smoking. False alarm? Nothing has ever scared me as much as the thought of being pregnant. ∎

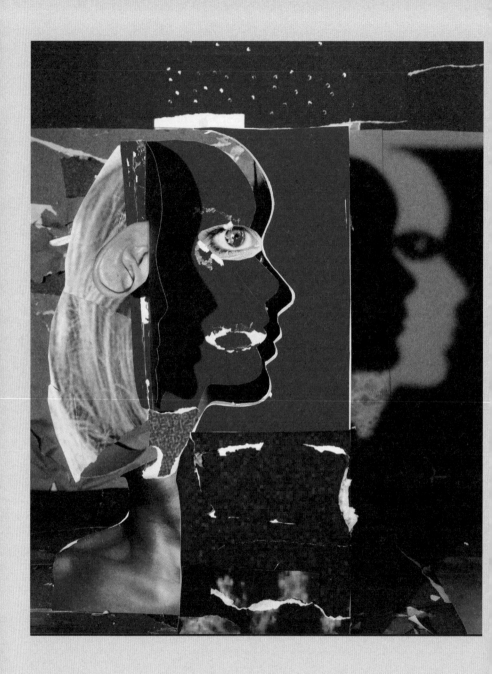

© DANIEL GORDON
Red Face III, 2011

FIRST LOVE

Gwendoline Riley

1

I used to look at houses like this one from the train: behind the ivy-covered embankment, their London brick, sash windows. That was on the Euston approach. The back of this flat – that is, the bedroom, the bathroom and Edwyn's study – looks out on the overground line, just past West Brompton.

I've been here for eighteen months but my boxes only recently came out of storage. Also in the consignment was my metal document case, half full of old papers, correspondence, a few photographs. I spent a long afternoon unpacking onto the new alcove shelves, deciding what to keep.

When I first moved in, and before that, when I came to visit (I think I came three times), I'd watch for Edwyn in the evenings: standing between the windows, eyeing the shadows out there. This is a short, curved terrace. Mullions and porch columns rib the way. The traffic might build at night but the pavements are never busy; the procession was thin down from Earl's Court, until at last there he'd be: blond hair poking from a black flat cap, grey overcoat flapping, his tatty rucksack on one shoulder. In his free hand he always held a bottle by the neck, wrapped tightly in its striped plastic bag.

Lately it's the round of coughing in the hallway that lets me know he's home. I go out and meet him, we have a cuddle, and then I look at the *Standard* while he gets changed. We don't talk much in the evenings, but we're very affectionate. When we cuddle on the landing, and later in the kitchen, I make little noises – little comfort noises – at the back of my throat, as does he. When we cuddle in bed at night, he says, 'I love you so much!' or 'You're such a lovely little person!' There are pet names, too. I'm 'little smelly puss', before a bath, and 'little cleany puss', in my towel on the landing after one; in my dungarees I'm 'you little Herbert!' and when I first wake up and breathe on him I'm his 'little compost heap' or 'little cabbage'. Edwyn kisses me repeatedly, and with great emphasis, in the morning.

There have been other names, of course.

'Just so you know,' he told me last year, 'I have no plans to spend my life with a shrew. Just so you know that. A fishwife shrew with a face like a fucking arsehole that's had . . . green *acid* shoved up it.'

'You can always just *get out* if you find me so contemptible,' he went on, feet apart, fists clenched, glaring at me over on the settee, 'You have to get behind the *project*, Neve, or get out.'

'What?'

'*Get . . . behind . . . the project . . . or . . . get out!*'

'What's "the project"?'

'The *project* is not winding me *up*. The *project* is not trying to get in my head and make me feel like *shit* all the time!'

He shouted this on his way to the bedroom. Twenty minutes later – hot-cheeked, I watched the time on the cooker clock – he came back.

'I don't suppose it would occur to you that I'm miserable . . .' he said, glumly but scornfully.

'But of *course*,' he went on, 'I *accept*, you've got a much more informed world view than I have! You've got a much deeper world view from collecting people's *glasses*. You've got a much wider knowledge of the world, from being on the *dole*, in the *North*, of *course*!'

There was a lot of shouting from him, back then. Long nights when his agitation, his flinches and side glances, would coalesce into a stronger force. Might you say we were coming to an accommodation, two people who'd always expected, planned, to live their lives alone? I'd never lived with anyone before, I had no idea what it might bring out in me. Certainly I remember feeling that it was his dream world, his symbol world, that we were dragged into during those first arguments, and it frightened me, being given – as I saw it – the part of a training dummy, outfitted in colours, slogans, that I could not see.

Edwyn's tall, over six feet, and these rooms do sometimes look too small for him. When we were rowing, especially, he'd often hunch himself up, round his shoulders, lower his head. Pacing, then pausing, as if in a spotlight, he'd soliloquise, restating his credo, which was – is – *It's freedom that counts.* He'd go on to wonder, haltingly, amazedly, at how he'd boxed himself in (ending up with me in his life, he meant), and when he did address me, it was abstractly, with strange conjectures, ruminations, about what I thought, who I was. 'I know you hate anyone who didn't grow up on benefits,' he'd say, and if I objected he took no notice, or didn't notice, he only continued, talking over me with mounting scorn: 'I know you loathe anyone who didn't grow up in *filth*, on benefits.'

I used to leave my body, in a way, while this went on. It was so incessant, his phrases so concatenated: there was no way in. These were thick, curtain walls.

Edwyn has said since that he feels it's me trying to annihilate *him.* Strange business, isn't it?

The difference between us, which I did try to keep in mind, was that he really did feel himself under threat back then. At just forty, he'd had serious heart trouble. An operation. He'd had to lose a lot of weight, stop smoking. Things had settled down by the time we met, but he told me he couldn't feel safe. Not ever again. He was also starting to suffer terribly with his joints. Fibromyalgia, as we later found out. 'I'm paying for something,' he'd snarl, cornered. Or sometimes he'd just sit and sob, and look up at me with frightened eyes when I sat next to him.

E dwyn grew up near Isleworth, an only child. He showed me the house once, the green he used to play on. We walk up that way most Saturdays, unless it's raining: taking the river path, crossing over at Putney. We hold hands, stop to feed the cruising ducks and coots, admire the doughtier dogs we see. I do like hearing about Edwyn when he was small. He was a worried little boy, he tells me, when he was three, and four, scared to leave his mother. But then he did used to race to wave at the trains that passed his garden. 'I was rushing towards life!' he says. Later, there was the Nature Club he founded at school, to which he would admit helpers, but no other members. Well, how could he trust them? One early romantic error stays with me, too: how he gave half an Easter egg each to the two girls in his class who liked him, terrified of alienating either one by preferring the other. 'No, they didn't think much of that,' he told me, earnestly, eagerly, 'I went from two girls to no girls!'

S undays have always been for work. I take the settee. Edwyn brings his papers down from his study. With the last of a glass of wine, and always a bunched-up tissue or two (in his office they call him 'The Kleenex Kid', he says), he sits bracketed to the dining table. Also before him is the church candle we light while we eat, and the tin the matchbox is kept in, labelled ALLUMETTES. Sometimes the curled fingers on his right hand lift like piano hammers, I suppose.

2

Y ears ago.
I remember: the sky's cold threat. Dishrag clouds, leaking light. And passing Garston: ramifying terraces. Wet slates. Smashed flags.

Lime Street was still under construction: plastic sheets patched the roof, and dripped; the concourse was diminished. My mother stood when she saw me, collected her bags. I stooped to kiss her cold, downy cheek and at that she bared her teeth, lifted her chin.

On the corner of Renshaw Street, the CASHINO was new. In its foil-ribbon window sat a white china tiger, gold-striped, long-necked, and with a clean-toilet gleam. Otherwise, here were the same immemorial chip shops, the sooty junk shops, with their racks of Crimplene costumes, mangy stoles. It was six months since my last visit. Back then my mother had linked arms with me on this stretch; she'd gripped my sleeve and leant in. I hadn't brushed her off, exactly, but it hadn't taken, and she didn't try it now. This was mid-December, a weekday afternoon. We walked quickly, pushing against the sniping wind. Or at least, I thought I was walking at her pace.

'Slow down! Slow down, Neve! Don't zoom off. I'm a pensioner now. I can't *sprint* everywhere!'

With a sort of proud helplessness she stopped and stood her ground; stoutly in her winter coat, which was ankle-length, grey-green, padded in rings. Her being 'a pensioner', 'an old *lady*, now', was a favoured new plea, back then. When she first retired, she said she felt lost. She said so often, if coyly. No one was interested, of course, and hence this new tack. Now she was kitted out. She had her *Saga* subscription, she told me, and she was vivacious on the subject of her new shopping trolley: 'No, Neve, it's brilliant, for a *pensioner!*'

'Shall I take some of those bags?' I said. 'What's in them?'

'Oh. Just, different things. Things you might be interested in. Since you *refuse* to come to the house I have to bring everything out with me, don't I?'

We were going to the cinema. There was a cafe on Bold Street where she wanted to get a drink first, she said, a new tea room, but as we turned the corner, she stopped again.

'*Oh* . . . shit,' she said, and then she stepped back into a doorway. 'What is it?'

'Tss . . . Someone I don't want to see. Old boyfriend.'

She pressed her shoulder against the shutter, turned further away.

'Really? When from?'

'A few years ago. Before Rodger.'

'Is he going to walk past?'

'No. I think he was going in a shop, but – wait a second. Just wait, Neve. Just wait, please . . . Okay, yes, come on, let's go quickly. Come on, and try and look engrossed in conversation. Look animated, Neve!'

She took my arm now, as we steamed away, so here was her face again, crowned with her red fleece cloche, banded by her purple-framed glasses, smiling purposefully up at me.

'This is nice,' I said, as we slid along the blond wood benches. I wiped a port in the steamed-up window, while she arranged her bags next to her, then her hat, her scarf, her too-big thermal gloves.

'Yes. I've been in here before. I don't usually like going in places on my own, places I don't know, but I'd been past a few times and it seems nice, doesn't it? Friendly.'

We ordered a pot of green tea each, and then both stood up again to take off our coats.

'So what boyfriend was that?'

'Oh. *Well* – it was after I moved to Catherine Street, do you remember I went out with that Jewish man, Simon, for a while, with the ponytail? No? Well I *did*. But after *him* I started seeing that man, Greg, and, yes, we went out a few times, oh but I could never ring him, you know, because he was *so* busy, I had to wait for him to ring *me*, or – big trouble. Big troub. Anyway – I didn't even like him very much. He repaired sash windows and he was quite open with me that he ripped people off. No shame about that. I've warned quite a few people since then, who've mentioned they're having their windows done, I say, Well, *whatever you do*, don't get Greg Martin to do it, he'll rip you off. Anyway, so he *did* ring me one afternoon and he dumped me, you see, and then even though I hadn't been out with him that often and I didn't like him very much I sort of – yes, I did get very upset about that, and ended up writing him this letter, which I regret now, so . . .'

'Oh dear.'

'Mm . . . Yes. And – no, he's not a very nice man, as it turned out, so . . .'

Her hair was chin-length then: thick, grey, limp. Behind her glasses her wide-set eyes looked frightened. She even looked frightened when the waitress set down our teapots, which were transparent and had a plunger.

'How do we get the tea out?' she whispered, as the girl moved off. 'Oh no! Come back!'

'I thought you'd been here before.'

'Oh, yes, well, I couldn't work it then either!'

Back in the summer she'd had a birthday M&S voucher she said she wouldn't use: did I want it? I did. She'd started her turn then as we crossed the floor to Hosiery: surrounded, as we were, by strange statuary. My mother blenched extravagantly at the gussied-up torsos, blinking hard like someone had flashed a torch in her eyes, saying she *couldn't* understand why *anyone* would buy, wear, matching underwear.

'Yes, it's *such* a relief I never, *ever* have to do *any* of that again,' she said. 'Yuck yuck *yuck*. Just – no. I can't even bear it in films now. I have to close my eyes!'

My mother went to the pictures a lot, back then, always to FACT, Liverpool's new cinema-gallery-cafe. I was often surprised by what she saw. I think she saw whatever they put on. As to what she thought of these films: hard to say. Her opinions were offered so cautiously. She might say something had been 'too long' or 'so violent!' I always felt terrible when she said, of something she'd looked forward to, and with only just a shade less brightness to her voice, that it had been: 'Not what I expected.' That even became a sort of sad catchphrase between Edwyn and me for a while, which I felt guilty about, slightly queasy about, sometimes. Once he asked me, 'Does everything your mother tries end in disaster?' Which made me feel desperate! But those were the stories she told me, so that's what I'd pass on. I didn't overdo that (I hope), but sometimes we swapped confidences. Once, when I first came to stay, when we were lying in bed. I don't know what prompted that discussion, of his mother on the loo.

'I used to hear these dreadful noises in the morning,' Edwyn said. And pleating his lips, and narrowing his eyes, to more precisely recall, so that his eyebrow quills stood rampant, he said, 'Gurgling and spluttering. Like bad plumbing. Which it was, I suppose. Her grossly over-functioning digestion! The thundering waterfall of her first piss! Terrifying. I thought bodies were terrifying. But then' – wistfully – 'puberty did its work – soon I couldn't wait to get up there!'

I told him:

'I have memories of my mum on the toilet, too. Noises in the night. She had IBS. Stress-induced. I heard her crying once and got up and found her sitting with her nightie all gathered up between her knees. She said, "Leave me, please, go back to bed Neve! Just leave me!" And there were these little splutters. In the morning I wondered if I'd dreamt it.'

'Oh dear. Poor old thing. "Just leave me." '

'Mmm . . . Well, she wasn't old then. She was my age. No. A bit older . . .'

I'd thought about that night when she got married again, too. She had a nasty hangover on her wedding day. When I got to her flat that morning she was quailing in a corner of the settee, and retching, and sobbing, a bucket with some Dettol in it at her feet.

In FACT my mother queued for our tickets, smiled as she showed her membership card. In the cinema, she moved along the row. Reaching the middle, she stopped and put all of her bags down on the seat to her left, between us, and then she started un-popping the poppers on her coat.

'What are you doing?'

'What?'

'Where am I going to sit?'

'Oh. No. I can't sit next to people.'

'Hey? We've come together. We always sit together . . .'

Here she showed her teeth again, looked cornered, angry.
'No. *No.* I always go on my own!'

How did it come to that?
Remember. Soon after they were married. That dusty old pub.
I was in town to see Kerrigan, but she'd been badgering me to give
her her old keys back, and I kept forgetting to post them. She was
going to meet Rodger and his friends for a drink, she said, in the
Crown. His 'artist friends', she called them, and they proved easy to
spot: a raucous group of men, in paint-scabbed fishermen's jumpers.
My mother wasn't quite sitting with them, though, but on a low
stool a few feet behind Rodger. She wore a familiar expression; too
eager, half sly, while no one spoke to her, or looked at her. She held
her empty half-pint glass up by her chin, and grinned hopelessly.
Kerrigan was waiting outside, I told her I couldn't stop, but still,
bravely, and to little effect, when I crouched down next to her, she
said, '*Everyone*, this is my *daughter.*'

It must be a dreadful cross: this hot desire to join in with people
who don't want you. This need to burrow in. But then – perhaps
I'm not one to talk. A year later, I was buying tickets for a preview
of Terence Davies's new film: in Liverpool, so I asked if she wanted to
come. 'Oh *yes*,' she said. 'And am I *allowed* to bring Rodger?'

Of Time and the City ends with fireworks dashing skywards,
pop-pop-pop, raining blue sparks over the Pier Head. The voiceover
says:

*Good night, ladies; good night, sweet ladies; good night, good night,
good night ...*

Following the producers up onto the stage, Davies took his bow
and I clapped hard. I was deeply moved by his flushed face, his
clasped hands. Here was an artist to the tips of his fingers, and he'd
been treated so shabbily, so disgracefully. He'd said somewhere, 'I lost
all hope.' Wouldn't you call that sickening?

Later, as we were standing to leave, as I was getting my bag from
under the seat, my mother said, 'Oh well it's all very well for him

going on about Liverpool, but he doesn't live here any more does he! And what's with that Donald Sinden voice?'

She was looking to Rodger.

'Don't be squalid, Mum. That was a beautiful work of art.'

She pulled a face now. An indignant face: mouth gaping. She put a hand to her chest.

'Squalid, *moi?*'

Rodger yawned, in his horse-ish way. Again, he didn't look at her, but pronounced, finally, as he zipped his coat. 'Not *art. Fart.*'

Rodger was a painter. He'd taught for years at the College of Art. Elsewhere, I'd asked my mother what she thought of his work, which hung throughout his house.

'Oh well I'm not *allowed* an opinion you see, not having been to *art school,*' she said. 'My opinion's worthless apparently, so . . . but I think they're all crap, yes. Absolute *crap,* so . . .'

'Have you told him that?'

'Oh he doesn't listen to what I say!'

Edwyn and I got married recently. Against both of our instincts, I think, but undertaken on his solicitor's advice, all part of putting his affairs in order. Everyone named in his previous will being dead, as he put it, and he wanted to take care of me. 'Do something useful,' he said. We went to the register office in Chelsea. A small, sunny room. An old wooden desk. There were no guests, just the two witnesses. Afterwards, outside, Edwyn had one of them take some photos on his phone. It was the hottest, driest day. Blazing sun. Nonetheless Edwyn had brought his umbrella out with him, so in each shot he's holding that, or leaning on it. In the last snap he's using it to point the way: a thin, black signal, down to the river for a drink.

3

That was in June. We didn't go away. We were due to drive down to Devon, but Edwyn's condition flared up, and he couldn't face the journey. Instead he stayed in bed for three days, then went back to work, desperately unhappy, difficult to soothe.

Those were a tough few weeks. Every day dawned humid, sticky. No cooling gusts on Cromwell Gardens. The thunder only proclaimed itself. I used to sit here with the windows open, the blinds down. Just me and the flies: quick-quick-slow, in the well of the room.

I had nowhere to be. In term time I'd be teaching on Wednesdays and Thursdays. (I didn't miss that.) And then on Friday afternoons I used to see a psychotherapist. Miss Moore – Amy – was based in Gospel Oak, in the Ford Road Serenity Centre, an old deaf school, I believe, now a warren of treatment rooms; long corridors lined with crowded noticeboards and empty coat pegs. I saw her for seven months, but gave my notice a few days before the wedding, finally overwhelmed by the powerfully childish sense of drag which had started to get into me, almost as soon as I sat down with her; before I sat down, when I set off from home.

I felt good as I left the last session, at least; delivered into my old silence, walking down the hill. I was glad to get the time back. Not incidentally, I was glad to save the money. I thought about the things I could do with it, as I waited for the tube, and then as I stood at the end of the carriage, swaying in the hot, rushing air.

Edwyn got in that night, as usual, at about half past eight. He called out, 'Phew, bloody hell!' as he climbed the stairs, and looked nice when he appeared on our landing, with his sunglasses dangling and his hair damp; his blue linen shirt untucked, but sticking to his round stomach and his back.

'Hello!' I said.

'What's all this?'

'It's detritus. I'm sorting things out.'

I stood up and took the wastepaper basket into the kitchen. Edwyn still had his rucksack on. He stood with his mouth slightly open, recovering from his walk.

'You're not going to leave that there are you?'

'No, I'm just emptying this.'

'Do you have to have the blinds down?'

'I do. But you can open them now.'

I stood at the sink, washing the dust from my nails. Soon enough Edwyn was behind me, looking at what I'd made for tea, giving it a creaturely sniff.

'Are you okay?' I said, 'Let's have a cuddle now.'

'Hm . . . Yes, I'm okay. I think I will have to avoid the Central line till the weather breaks, though.'

'Oh dear. Yes, go a different way. Poor thing. Prr prr. You smell nice.'

'Don't I smell horrible and sweaty?'

'No, I like it. Prr prr. Lovely Mr Pusskins.'

'Lovely *Mrs* Pusskins! Prr prr.' ∎

Melissa Lee-Houghton

The Price You See Reflects the Poor Quality of the Item and Your Lack of Desire for It

We sleep with minds of black and white confetti—
the fragmented thoughts and brain cells coalesce, dance—
we pose as anarchists, we develop Alzheimer's
just to lose ourselves within ourselves. Are you seriously telling me
this is your best analysis? The dying stall and drink from virally
   infected cups, and go out
with wet hair to catch pneumonia, because it's better that way. I walk
   away from you
without glancing back, in case you see in me something I don't.

Don't worry, man, I've been tamed.
I was raised in a home in a gun-toting vacuum,
where self-expression repeatedly hit its head
until its brains secreted all my secrets
dashing out blood on the carpet. You're really
far too intelligent, and spiteful, and you have me, love/hate if you've
   the right.
Cut it with something cheap, stretch it out, and sell me for a high
   reach price.

The sun kisses and kisses and kisses
and sucks on my lycra tongue
that sizzles with a saturnine thirst and Captain Morgan's—
I really want you to buy handcuffs, I tell him,
but he says, 'no, you'll scream. You'll scream and you'll scream
until someone comes.' I say, 'no one
ever comes when someone screams.'

It's very hard to work with ethical principles when dealing with
(another) lunatic
artist. I've invested a lot in this and want a high return;
I'm generous because it validates my existence—
we should wait for the end fucking in cars rolling backwards,
and liberate our friends by telling them
everything we disliked about them or their parents.
Another door slams in another convex hole. I dive into bed listening
for gunshots.

I was in a queue at the bank, disabled, visibly, with a cheque in
another name,
and someone remarked, 'she's not fit for purpose' and I will
remember their face in the afterlife, so I know whose tea to piss in. I
shatter
all the mirrors in the house with my
awful, ragdoll looks and temperament. I will look good for you
as you're easily disappointed. Haven't seen the moon, any moon, for
weeks.
Haven't seen the sea in months, but I'm not dying yet so it doesn't
call me.

I can't see your absence so maybe it doesn't exist. If I
live like this again I'll baste my achievements in fat monetary value.
I'll sell my piss and blood and eggs and avoid drugs tests.
I'll keep racing along to rock and roll and spin out through time-
zones, those
limitless years of suffering limits. I regress

THE PRICE YOU SEE REFLECTS THE POOR QUALITY OF
THE ITEM AND YOUR LACK OF DESIRE FOR IT

to nineteen ninety-eight where my sister leaves her white powder in
the bedroom drawer.
I don't know what it is so I snort it and get high and still don't know
what it is.

In '02 I drank cheap champagne
in the back room of the addiction hostel
and imagined my own dead body dragged through the nonchalant
halls backwards.
The boys gave me enough to see me through the long nights.
I needed so much and couldn't have it—
and no one wanted to share in my euphoria or hurt—
now I need to always risk losing something to feel safe.

When the lights go out—sometimes my mother sits and hates me for
several minutes,
but sometimes, just sometimes, she can't think up a passive-aggressive
response
within the time it takes to change topic.
She always said I like the sound of my own voice,
so now I bask in it, and light up.
And I write in it, and I hear it in my sleep
and it tells me I'm a good bad girl of innocent intent.

There's nothing worse than wearing a yellow tie and bright blue suit
except of course
wearing it in public and being photographed for facebook.
Only kidding. But seriously. I mellowed out but not overly. These are
the pitfalls

of living in the twenty-first century you better believe it boy.
Our sanity depends on saying the right thing at the right time
and woe betide the woman who says 'this'll take the edge off it' or
'you'll be ok in no time if you do what I say'. She wants community

to make her sins ok. History relies on our ineffability and
manic delusion and deletion, and technology that will be
defunct and unsupported in time, so lie down in my bed and
hate language with me, and suck it
up out of my mouth. Bite down on it, baby—
we are sleeping now like imbeciles. There's no need to imagine
    ourselves
up to no good, just better to be in the moment, and not worry about
    it.

When I was sixteen I would jump the intercity met.
How foolish to stay out of dodge,
to believe anyone is free, having a free pass at living,
heroin has given me twelve years of realism and acne,
I shudder at the thought of being clear,
conventional, mapped like a school atlas with a way in and a way out.
I never suffered more than now.

That's no one's fault until my brain decides otherwise
when paranoid or high. No one wants to see my
hesitant circus act, the nihilists
lick their salted lips, run their tongues over dirty teeth.
When it sucks just stick to the facts—in ten years we'll have nothing
    more to talk about but

the odd stage directions punctuating our lives, that no one read or
interpreted.
Baby, you landed on your feet. But I'll kill you.

Trapped in a little girl's forgetfulness I beg
and the abacus that infers my life is fettering away
now fades. If I don't live forever I don't see why I can't
do anything I want. Jump ship. Lie in court.
Become a more mysterious person. Leave a blank note.
Scream and wail. Mourn the lives of everyone I ever met whether
dead or not.
Look back and see you turn away, and never do anything again but
think on it.

RAQQA ROAD:
A SYRIAN ESCAPE

Claire Hajaj

The morning Helin walked out to die, she dressed carelessly in a loose T-shirt and jeans. She did not brush her hair. The room she shared with three others in a Beirut tenement stank of sweat. Her daughter Lulu sang on the bed, small hands waving, weaving stories.

A brutal summer's day was waking in Lebanon; the early heat rolled over the city. Lulu rested heavy in her arms – Lulu who'd celebrated her first steps with bruises from blind collisions. Lulu whose fading eyes saw less and less of the sky each day, for whom the birds were now only a darkening blur as they swept overhead.

Women thronged the roadside; old and young, hair tucked under hijabs or straggling in hennaed ponytails. Some hoisted sleeping infants, expressions blank with practiced appeal. Others thrust out boxes of sweets and creased photographs, trying to catch the traffic as it whirred past.

Syrians. Their eyes slid past each other, as if recognition carried mutual horror. But Helin could read the stories written there, in the shared language of dispossession. It described the future racing towards her: begging, selling bubblegum at pitiless crossroads, trading her body in mould-streaked bedrooms under the flicker of neon lights.

She walked down the long road towards the United Nations High

Commissioner for Refugees. The UNHCR headquarters in Lebanon stand white and tall on Beirut's southern flank of Jnah, near the sea. In Arabic, Jnah means 'wing'. To the thousands of Syrians making their weary pilgrimage here, the word conjures sensations of flying, the illusion of open skies.

She rounded the corner and saw the queue: a human tail winding back from the gate. Children escaped, laughing as they chased each other along its length. Lulu's head twisted towards them, following the noise. The adults stared ahead, vacant, like machines on stand-by, waiting for a signal to wake up.

Helin's feet stopped at the kerb's edge. Land Cruisers breezed past her towards the entrance. The heat from the engines brushed her face. She hesitated, breathing, her chest slippery from Lulu's clinging heat.

That touch evoked a vivid memory – of another long walk, nine months ago in al-Raqqah, where Islamic State banners were flying.

On that morning she'd dressed carelessly too, prepared for death but praying for life. She'd thrown Lulu's things into a suitcase, feeling watched, their house besieged by silence.

Silence had become her greatest enemy; it had swallowed the land. Silence had claimed Raqqa's markets where once people had eaten *manquish* and swapped stories. It had occupied the house where once she and Rami would relax on the sofa together, drinking tea. Silence ruled the wasteland outside the city, ringed by checkpoints and shallow graves.

Lulu was the only remedy for silence. Seven months old, she was a wellspring of sound. Sickness had turned her skin to paper and sharpened her bones; but still she sang, and laughed and cried, her face astonished at the power of sound pouring out of her.

The baby had been Rami's gift, a longed-for child born far away in Aleppo as bombs fell. *I'm a war bride,* Helin would tell herself – a Kurdish girl who had fallen for an Arab boy as war fell on them, guillotine-swift.

One day, the uprising against Bashar al-Assad was just an

argument over coffee or a headline in a news bulletin; the next, Helin's street was bristling with armed convoys. Soon, sentries patrolled the pavement. Helin's brother watched as he smoked his evening cigarette on the balcony. They shouted up to him: *You up there! Get back inside!* Life's choices narrowed. Helin's short skirts had to go; for the first time in her life, she put on the hijab.

Assad's bombs came next, sun-bright flashes followed by dull thuds, shaking the air like thunderstorms at noon. *This is not Syria*, Helin's neighbours whispered among themselves. *Our own government wants us dead.* It was astonishing, apocalyptic, as if the world was already finished, its few survivors abandoned.

Helin's family tried to back away from the frontline; they sought shelter in north Aleppo. That's where she met Rami – charming Rami who didn't notice Helin's scoliosis-damaged spine, kind Rami who helped old women carry heavy bags home, who didn't care that Helin was a Kurd. Their relationship crossed Syria's new barricades; it split Helin from her family. In Aleppo, wrote T.E. Lawrence, *the races, creeds, and tongues of the Ottoman Empire met and knew one another in a spirit of compromise.* But compromise was Aleppo's first casualty. Arab and Kurd, Christian and Muslim, Sunni and Shia – the days of tea and backgammon were done; the tables were overturned. In the heat of universal rebellion, her family's *no* made Helin more determined to say *yes. Yes*, she said, when he asked her to marry him. *Yes* she said again, when he offered to take her to Raqqa, seventy miles to the east.

Lulu was then just three weeks old. Helin's pregnancy had been a sudden wonder, a joy that for a while had pushed war into retreat. But war soon pressed in again. Aleppo had been drained of food; Rami's vegetable cart was empty. She cooked rice and ate bread in their small apartment, each meal more expensive than the last.

Her labour came early; she delivered in Aleppo's maternity hospital, its walls shaking with bomb blasts. Lulu was born weak. She needed an incubator, and Helin needed rest; but these were luxuries from the past. A harried doctor wrapped Lulu up and rushed them out of the door, desperate for every extra bed.

Raqqa would save them, Rami promised. No bombs fell in Raqqa; it was safe, protected by the Free Syrian Army. But the landscape troubled Helin; it was flat, barren, the mighty Euphrates shrivelled. She was lonely in their new house. Rami became stressed, and more distant. Each time they set out to market, they'd hear gunfire's distant rattle. *Who's fighting?* she'd ask Rami. *Who knows?* he'd answer.

Then, on a cool day in Raqqa's spring, they knew. A banner flew above the market centre. It read: THE ISLAMIC STATE HAS THE VICTORY.

That was the end of walking, the end of markets and *manquish*. Instead, there were edicts. No talking loudly. No showing skin. Black over the face. Black shoes. The women stopped living: they became ghosts.

Soon the bombs returned, blasting the earth. *Americans*, Rami said. *Or Russians. Or the French.* The bombs were their own single nation; wherever they came from they fell without discrimination – on medical centres and schools, clinics, on the municipal sports stadium and shopping markets.

But Helin had an even greater worry. *Look at Lulu*, she appealed to Rami. *Something's wrong.* The baby's eyes didn't focus; she seemed to look through her mother, not at her.

It's the water, he replied, frustrated. The taps were running red, like an omen. Bombs had fractured the city's pipes. Dirty water flooded out of their daughter's small body in diarrhoea, withering her in front of their eyes.

'Why didn't you just leave?' I can't help asking Helin, later. She shakes her head, and I suddenly remember why some questions can't be answered. I learned it in Baghdad, ten years ago, when every man approaching a mosque, every car slowing at a checkpoint, could have been rigged with explosives. The wonder was not that people ran but that they stayed. It's a fatal human flaw; we burrow when we should flee, we cling to our homes until the last barrier is breached, until running is the only option left.

For Helin, the breach came when Rami vanished. It began with a broken promise. Each day, he would come home by two in the afternoon – not a minute later. Otherwise she'd go crazy with worry, stuck in the house, listening to Lulu chatter and babble. The last time, he was heading out to buy bread and rice for dinner. He stood framed in the doorway, light flooding past. *Don't open the door to anyone until I get back.* And then the door closed, shutting her in.

This time he wasn't back at two o'clock, nor at three, nor at four.

As the sun began to fall, fear gripped Helin around the throat. She called the police and then the hospital. Had anyone matching his description been found? No one, they said. At last she pulled on her niqab, the long black gloves and thick dark robe, the black scarf stifling her face. She pulled Lulu into her arms and did what she'd promised never to do – she stepped out into the red glare of sunset and walked towards the city's outskirts. There, beyond the streets and the training camps, the executed dead lay unburied. She stood at Raqqa's edge and looked out over emptiness. It stared back at her, giving no sign.

The sky was darkening. It was not permitted for a woman to be out alone. She tried to pray, but her mouth was dry. Lulu lay quiet on her shoulder, worn out by the heat, silenced at last. Helin looked inside herself for grief, but found none. There was no room for anything but fear.

That night she lay awake. Every sense strained for the first echo of feet pounding the steps, fists at the door. In the silence of Raqqa, women were forbidden to speak aloud in public. But they still talked, in whispers. *When they come for you, it's not just one man. They each take a turn before they kill you.* Lulu was asleep next to her. Helin curled around her daughter, wrapping her in a human cocoon. But it was just an illusion; she could not protect her own child. Pregnancy had worsened Helin's scoliosis; each step was now a painful act of will. If they came, she would not be able to run.

By the time dawn broke, she knew her courage was gone: she could not stand another night. Rami had left some emergency cash; she pulled it from the hiding place, tucking it inside a pack of diapers, loading a suitcase with Lulu's bottles and a handful of clothes. She called a neighbour and told him about Rami's disappearance. *You're right*, he said. *You should go. Now.*

He picked her up in his car minutes later. The first checkpoint was a mile outside of town. Helin lay down, huddled on the back seat. But a hundred metres from the checkpoint her neighbour's nerve failed; he pulled up. He opened the car door. *Out*, he told her.

The open door filled her with horror. *I can't*, she said, clutching the seat. He shook his head. *If they find out we're not related, we're both dead.*

He left her there, on the road leading out of Raqqa. Helin started to walk, pulling her suitcase over the stony sand. Her niqab was hot and heavy; her black gloves slippery with sweat. Lulu coughed over her shoulder. The checkpoint was a red line across the sand, the Islamic State fighter barely a shadow through Helin's black veil. She held Lulu out, showing him the baby's paper skin and hollow eyes. *She's dying*, she whispered, hushing her voice so as not to anger him. *She needs a proper hospital.*

There was a pause, filled only with her breath – too loud, she thought, terrified, too urgent. Then he held something out to her: a paper, its marks unreadable. *Take this to the next checkpoint*, he said.

The next checkpoint was two miles away. Her back ached, hobbling each step as her feet twisted on sharp stones. At every step she thought only of Lulu, safety and Lulu – the two words merged in her mind. She clutched the mujahid's paper as it fluttered against her fingers in the hot wind. Was it their release, or their death warrant? There was no way to know. Prayer was useless, and so were plans. She just had to keep walking.

The second checkpoint brushed her through with barely a glance. But the fighters at the third one were standing on the road as she approached, unmoving in the heat. Terror returned, cold and mocking. *The mujahid called ahead to warn them*, it said. *They're waiting for you.*

Clasping Lulu against her, she held out the piece of paper. The sun shone through it as the fighter read. She held her breath, Lulu's sweat soaking through to Helin's skin. Then he jerked his head. *Go*, he told them, stepping out of her path.

And suddenly, she stood on the road outside Raqqa, beyond the occupation.

Buses were coming and going; she boarded one and bought a ticket. *To Aleppo*, she told the driver. The volume of her voice shocked her, after months of speaking in whispers. *There's nothing in Aleppo*, he replied. *Everyone who can has gone.*

He was right: Aleppo was empty, a siege zone. The rebel soldiers who'd patrolled Helin's streets were either dead or pinned down. Assad's men had advanced, vengeful and encircling. Cafes and shops were closed, the streets were rubble. *Afrin*, people told her. *The Kurds all went to Afrin.*

Afrin. Helin knew it, Syria's Kurdish heartland, which had recently broken from Assad to declare self-rule. As she boarded another bus, she pictured its hills and olive trees – green like the uniforms of its young soldiers now fighting against the Islamic State in nearby Kobane.

But that was before. This Afrin was different; it had swelled, like a river in full flood. As the bus pulled up at the central station she held on to the open door, terrified of being swept away. Thousands had come, fleeing Aleppo and Kobane and the carnage of nearby sieges. The streets were thronged; they smelled of violence. Helin had a family photograph, and nothing more. She tried to catch people as they raced past. *Do you know them? Did they come here?* One old woman stopped; she looked at Lulu, asleep on Helin's shoulder. *Do you have anywhere to stay?* she asked. Helin shook her head, exhausted. *Stay with me*, the woman said. *Just for a while.*

The worst thing about war, Helin told me once, is not knowing friends from enemies. Afrin was full of strangers; she felt eyes crawling over her as she paced the streets, searching. She became suspicious of sympathy. She feared the Kurdish soldiers, boys and girls in green, marching through Afrin's parks. They might be heroes, but they drew bombs like carrion draws flies. Turkish artillery started shelling the city, blasting the resurgent Kurdish nationalism. The Islamic State was approaching from the south-east, with mortars and missiles.

The world is dissolving. Helin found no trace of her family. She held Lulu at night, her mind pounding with urgency: what should they do next? Lulu's bones were growing through her skin. A doctor had waved his finger in front of her unresponsive eyes. *She has bigger problems than diarrhoea,* he'd told Helin. *I think she's going blind.*

Lebanon: that was the word on everyone's lips. The border was still open – but not for long. She sat with the old woman in her stifling kitchen after the doctor's diagnosis, Lulu like a wilted flower in her arms. *Better try the UNHCR,* the old woman said, eventually. *They're the only ones who can help her.* The UN was everyone's great hope; God had failed; the UN's miracles were all that remained.

Helin arrived at Beirut's Charles Helou bus station in September 2014 – one among a million Syrians. Refugees lay over the country like a blanket; from the vineyards of the Bekaa to the shores of the restless Mediterranean. Syrian children begged along Beirut's winding Corniche, blacking shoes and selling roses. The bullet-riddled skeleton of the Holiday Inn loomed over them, a memento mori from Lebanon's own violent past.

The Kurdish bus driver offered Helin a room in his house: two families squashed into crowded bedrooms. The next morning, she queued with hundreds of others to register with the UNHCR. *Refugee.* She'd known refugees in Syria, from other countries' wars. She'd pitied them. Now the tables were turned. Now the tide of Syrians was so vast and relentless that all the world's pity could drown in it.

Lulu's first medical appointment in Lebanon brought only bad news. She was diagnosed with severe cataracts, worsened by malnutrition in the womb and during infancy. *She has a one-year window for an operation,* the doctor told Helin. *After that the blindness will be permanent.*

Helin still remembers that diagnosis; how her arms went out, as if to push it away. *If I had left sooner. If I had eaten more.* She had failed in motherhood's first duty – to nourish and protect the child inside her.

Lulu's operation would cost $10,000 in Beirut's prohibitively expensive private health system. Helin sold her last possessions, haggling and pleading with aid organizations to make up the rest. Travelling weekly to the UNHCR, she begged them for help. Either treat Lulu – or send her onwards, to Europe or some other kind haven, where her treatment would be free.

At the resettlement interview, the UNHCR official asked Helin: *Where is her father? Dead*, she replied as Lulu sang in her lap. They asked to see his death certificate. She remembers looking down at her empty hands. It was her worst moment since Rami vanished – a reminder that he could still be alive somewhere, suffering.

Without any proof of Rami's death, Lulu could not be resettled abroad. War had fractured thousands of marriages; too many frantic parents had come to the UN on their fruitless search for missing children and partners. The UNHCR tried to explain – gently, inured to despair. Yes, it was hard. Yes, papers got lost in the maelstrom of flight. But new dramas were flooding across the border every day, ten thousand at a time. Less than half of the nearly 500,000 Syrians judged in urgent need of resettlement would ever board a flight. Those few needed to have their papers in order.

Another blow was in store: there was no money for Lulu's eye operation. The UNHCR was running on empty. They needed $250 million to subsidise doctor's visits, vaccines, nutrition services and medicine for a million refugees – but only $53 million had been donated. One in every four people in the country was a refugee. Lebanon's public hospitals were overwhelmed with Syrian patients; money was short for everything, from chemotherapy to dialysis.

Helin refused to accept this equation, angrily denying its logic. She had come so far, three hundred miles; she had cast herself and her daughter into the void, trusting that someone would catch them.

Now, the weekly journey to the UNHCR felt longer than three hundred miles. Helin would sit outside their offices, Lulu on her lap, shaking off remonstrations from the gate guards. *I won't move*, she told them. *Not until the head of the UNHCR comes to talk to me.*

No one came. Lulu celebrated her first birthday; she learned to walk; she ran without seeing, wounding herself. Eyes began to follow them in their shared room – narrow, speculating. Helin thought they held silent admonitions: *If you're short of money why don't you beg, like the rest? Or earn your keep on your back?*

The weight of those eyes dragged her to a dark realisation: there are no miracles and no saviours. She had run from danger but danger had tracked them. As she sat by the towering UNHCR building, a mad notion took hold of her – what would happen if she left Lulu there, alone? Orphans went to the top of every UN list; orphans could get exceptions. The idea infected her: by the time the doctor confirmed that Lulu's eyesight was nearly extinguished, it had spread like a sickness, distorting her thoughts. She saw herself as her daughter's enemy, blocking her way to freedom.

In June 2015, nine months after her escape from Raqqa, Helin stood for the last time at the entrance to the UNHCR in Beirut, watching UN staff directing refugees inside the gate. Her body felt light with rage. The UN staff disintegrated; memories flooded through her; the silence of an empty home, red lines across a desert road, stony miles with a dry mouth and sweating palms, the chaos of bombs, Lulu's blind singing.

In slow motion she saw the UNHCR staff turn towards her, alarmed. And she realised she was screaming, holding Lulu out. *Look at her! Look at her.* She felt tears; she closed her eyes against them, forgetting even Lulu, forgetting everything except this long road to failure. A car came around the corner, accelerating towards her. She took a last step, into its path.

E ight months later, Helin and I are having lunch at the Beirut Souks. Our young waiters have friendly American accents honed by satellite TV. Around us, marble archways and high-end stores stretch out across the barely remembered Green Line, which divided Christian and Muslim neighbourhoods.

My six-year-old daughter compares her glasses with Lulu's new ones, two giant pink rings hugging her face. My daughter laughs. *They're spooky.* Lulu peers through them, puzzled by the cheeseburger magnified hugely by the lenses.

My husband asks Helin if she'd like something else. *You choose,* she says. She still looks at him as the saviour, the one with all the answers. It was his car that screeched to a halt in front of her. He came home that day, ashen-faced. *At the far end of hysteria,* he described her to me, sitting on the sofa with our daughter in his arms.

Helin herself remembers little from the moment her feet left the pavement. There are only impressions: the scream of tires, the consuming thud of her heart, someone taking Lulu from her, a blurred face asking her questions.

I doubt my husband will ever forget how he felt standing there – the weight of a hundred pairs of eyes on him, each holding their own painful story. It's the old dilemma of the too-fortunate living amid the desperate: is this the right one to help? There are too many children selling roses at midnight, too many women holding out papers and infants, watched discreetly by men from roadside corners. They turn us into moral cowards; the more reasons they give us to stop, the faster we walk, and the tighter we cling to the belief that we have some useful, urgent destination.

But the choice Helin gave my husband was simple: stop, or drive over her. Two days later, he called Helin with news. He'd contacted INARA, a charity set up by journalist Arwa Damon to provide surgery to war-wounded children. They would arrange Lulu's operation and provide her with aftercare.

'Who will pay?' Helin asked. My husband didn't tell her that he and INARA had already started fundraising, that calls and emails were flying across continents, rattling the tin. 'Don't worry,' he told her. 'It's free.'

Lulu's surgery took place three weeks later at the American University of Beirut Medical Center. INARA sent a skilled social worker, Layal, to counsel Helin through the recovery process. Dozens of Syria's war wounded have already come through INARA's doors: Layal had seen children burned in bomb attacks, limbs infected by botched repairs in Syria's blasted hospitals, children without hands, without faces. She'd sat with parents through long surgeries and painful recoveries. 'Even grief can become a habit,' Layal told me. When so much has gone wrong, it's hard to accept life when suddenly it goes right. But the children are more resilient. 'Hope comes naturally to them,' she said. 'And despair to us.'

Later, Helin and I sip tea on my balcony watching the Mediterranean Sea redden below. Spires of Beirut's resurrected downtown pierce the sunset. Once we would have been looking at rubble and corpses; once this, too, was the front line of a civil war.

Lulu sits beside her mother, mimicking with her hands; I find myself wondering what Syria will look like in thirty years. Will Aleppo rise again, in gleaming spirals of steel and glass? And if that day comes, will it still feel like home to Aleppo's people? Syria's losses haunt Helin – the deep, tugging ache of an amputated limb. Almost every refugee I speak to describes that same backwards pull. They can only move forward by a painful shedding: memories, identities, old dreams, old loves.

In two days Helin will start another journey – at Beirut's Rafic Hariri International Airport, boarding a flight to Sydney. Those phone calls and emails raised more than money: the UNHCR made an exception, sending Helin's case to officials in Beirut's Australian embassy. Australia immediately offered her asylum.

The airport's flight path skims the coast by my house. That evening we watch the planes, the low sun dazzling on their bellies. I ask Helin what she will do first, when she opens the door of her new house.

It makes her smile. 'Lie on the couch,' she says. 'Cuddle Lulu. And start to forget.' But she then corrects herself, shaking her head. 'I don't want to forget. It's like we were stuck in quicksand and someone pulled us out.'

Lulu sits beside her, mimicking her mother with her hands; at the word *pull* she leans forward, embracing happy armfuls of air. 'I look at her when she sleeps,' Helin says. 'I wonder what her life would have been like; why any child should be forced to live that way.'

I have no answer for her, no explanation for the arbitrary winds that have blown through her country and her people, scattering them like leaves. Why should Helin be saved, and not her parents, not her husband, not the millions without a ticket to safety in their pocket? The obscenity of it, the multitude of souls cast carelessly onto a roulette wheel. Helin will always be haunted by the ghost of another life – one where she stepped in front of a different car, arriving at the UNHCR a little earlier, or a few minutes too late.

I hope Helin forgets that cold shiver of a near miss. I make her promise to leave it behind, before my husband waves them onto their Emirates Airlines flight, their suitcase bumping up the gangway. Next morning I check my watch: Helin's key should be turning in her new door. Later my phone pings: Helin, sending me word on Facebook from Sydney – two thumbs up, and a heart. ■

AUTHOR'S NOTE: INARA (Arabic for 'ray of light') is a non-profit organisation founded in 2014 to provide Syrian child refugees with life-transforming surgery. INARA operates across Lebanon, which currently shelters over one million Syrian refugees.

© DANIELA YOHANNES
No Poor Among Us, 2013

AFRICA'S FUTURE HAS NO SPACE FOR STUPID BLACK MEN

Pwaangulongii Dauod

1

Boy, that night was energy.

2

It was the night that I'd last see C. Boy, for a couple of weeks later, in March, he would be found dead in his backyard. The night was full of energy. The kind of energy that Africa needs to reinvent itself. Fierce. Electrifying. Full.

3

13 January 2015. On the second anniversary of the day and year Nigeria signed the Same Sex Marriage Prohibition Act into law, I honoured an email invitation from C. Boy to attend a secret party

for homosexuals he was hosting in a nightclub in Kaduna. The invite mentioned coming along with a partner who had enough discipline to keep a secret. 'The partner may be "straight" but must not be homophobic; an artist is preferable,' it emphasised. And beneath it was an NB that read 'There will be a brainstorming session on the word "AFRO-MODERNISM". We are giving it a new meaning. Kindly pre-study the word.'

It sounded like a great idea, so I called a lesbian friend (a photographer-cum-designer-cum-blogger) and we headed to the nightclub, somewhere in Kaduna South, in a district known as Barnawa.

The year before, I had attended a dance concert curated by C. Boy in Gombe. It was meant to be a *fundraiser*, through ticket sales, for the gay club he had just founded. Though the event was a public show, the intention behind it was kept secret except for a few of his cronies. I was one of them. But it eventually turned out to be a total flop. It poured all day, and the hired loudspeakers and the improvised stage already set up in the middle of a primary-school field were destroyed. Later that night, we sat in the lobby of a cheap motel and talked over bottles of beer about the loss of funds put into the concert. He kept smiling in his seat, constantly rubbing his moustache, and joining the conversation in monosyllables.

C. Boy was from Adamawa, in north-eastern Nigeria. His father had sent him to Zaria to study engineering at the Ahmadu Bello University, because he 'wanted his family to produce the first engineer in his home town'. But C. Boy had another plan: on arriving in Zaria he deferred his admission, rented a flat off campus and began learning software applications, website creation and concept development, all by himself. He did this until the following term, when he began his classes. But still, he wasn't excited. Most of the time, he was out of Zaria, travelling by night bus to far-away Port Harcourt to visit his lover, a boy he had met and fallen in love with through Facebook just before he was granted admission to university. 'My father was thinking I was the "obedient" budding engineer from his home town. But leaving his house was leaving his ways and dreams. Everyone got his drives. My father's is not mine,' he said to a group of students in his apartment one Sunday morning in 2013. We were having a Sunday brunch.

It was from his numerous visits to Port Harcourt that he found a gay community and thought of founding one himself in Zaria. So, that night in the lobby of the motel, he mourned the loss of another chance to fund the club. A club he held so dear.

That day, as I headed to the nightclub, I wondered why he sat in that lobby as though he had just lost someone close to him, and also why this particular party was not a ticketed event.

11 p.m. We arrived late. A friend dropped us off a street away from the club, and we begged him to return for us at five in the morning. He drove off, and we crossed the road to our destination. My partner led the way; I walked behind, carrying her camera, a notepad and a spare pullover. The harmattan was a bitch.

I swear. The bouncers at the doorway would scare the hell out of John Cena. They allowed us entrance when we showed an e-copy of the invite on my friend's phone.

There was a check-in desk in the hall. We were issued tags. Mine read, WE ARE THE FUTURE DEMOCRACY, and hers, IN OUR FATHER'S HOUSE, THERE ARE MANY LOVES. WE CHANT IT COS IT'S SO. Soon we walked inside to join the party.

C. Boy, our host, saw us from where he was standing by the DJ's booth and started toward us, smiling. His jeans, dyed dreadlocked hair and dashiki matched the colour of wine in the glass in his hand: burgundy.

The party was pulsating. It was a festival of energy, of music, of hair, of ideas, of gays, of happiness, of fashion. Of language, love, meaning. A festival of dreams and assertion.

My friend headed to the bar for a drink, and I jumped to the dance floor to rock lost-but-found folks and long-time brothers.

4

I first met C. Boy on 14 September 2012. He had been invited to perform at a poetry slam I was hosting on the rooftop of a house in Samaru, a neighbourhood in Zaria. Apart from stealing the show with his epic spoken-word performance, he got in a fight with a guy who had performed a poem that mocked homosexuals. He was mad like a bull that night. He would have killed the guy if not for the crowd that fought to restrain him. After the event, I recall, he sat apart from everyone in a yellow plastic chair and wept like a child. We became friends and soon got to know each other well: I am bisexual, he's homosexual.

C. Boy was the engineering student who could recite all the scholars in the humanities and their theories by heart. He had read the postcolonial texts and hated Walter Rodney's theories. I heard rumours that he had dropped out. 'Yes, I left engineering,' he told me. 'It wasn't a dropout, it's a changeover.'

Cliché, but the true nature of things: if you are found to be gay in Nigeria, you are on your way to prison, to rot away for the next six hundred and something weeks of your fucking life. And that's if you're lucky. Because you don't always get it, you can't always get it. Why? Because you are the demon that needs to be exorcised, lynched, stoned to death, hacked to death, burned to death, beaten to death, or done something to death. It doesn't matter how: you must die, before the law manages to stroll by to see your predicament. So, to avoid rotting away in prison or getting killed, you take to secret love and/or a pretend heterosexual orientation.

All over Nigeria, your kind is harassed and troubled daily. From Bauchi to Zamfara, from Kano to Yobe, from Kaduna to Borno, from Abuja to Benue, Kogi, Plateau and Lagos, from Warri to Benin, all the way to Nnewi, your kind suffers public thrashings, stonings and judgements. They do. We do.

It was to reinterrogate this narrative that C. Boy dropped out of school. It sounded like a crazy and risky idea for a 24-year-old to be leaving school for such a project, but C. Boy had guts. All he wanted was to found a club that served LGBT people, a space where they could network and find expression. A warm brotherhood for people of 'like passions' living in a society that demonises them. 'The club has to be an energetic underground space,' he once told me. 'They don't see us, but we exist. It has to be this way until the crazies in the government reverse that fucking law.'

21 October 2013, on his birthday, he founded the club by hosting a party of fifteen people (all gay) in the small flat off campus that he was still renting. He named it Party BomBoy (PBB).

5

This party brought to eleven the number of PBB events I had attended. From concerts, open mikes, readings, exhibitions and symposia, retreats and picnics to poetry slams.

6

The DJ scratched the groove and it seemed the roof would come down on us. Highlife is energy. My dancing partner at the moment was Maima, a writer from Lokoja. We rocked on. Two prisoners just let loose. Energy.

It was that time in every party, that time when it turns into a whirlwind. Booze and Afrobeat-enhanced ecstasy. That time when you lose your partner to the crowd, indifferent to the loss because you are absorbed in rocking with someone else. Everybody becomes generous with his partner, his spirit, his smells and his sweat.

C. Boy and I left the party to chat a bit. Two months earlier, I had told him that I was writing about the gay movement in northern Nigeria and needed an interview with him. So, since we both were so overscheduled, we had arranged a brief interview for that night.

We sat by the doorway, on the seats by the check-in desk. We talked, sharing cigarettes and drinks. He appeared fatigued and slimmed-down. The bags under his eyes sagged in an unsettling way. 'I am just battling depression, but trust me always, your nigga is fine,' he said when I tried to find out what was wrong. We laughed; pecked each other. I asked for his permission to record our interview and he sipped his drink, smacked, and nodded. 'You are asking that? Come on, dude; don't make this nigga feel like a celeb. Come on.'

When C. Boy founded PBB he never knew the extent to which the club would play important roles in the lives of young men and women like him. He had only thought of using the money he made from designing games and websites to support and house in his small flat in Zaria seven to ten people who had been displaced because of their sexual orientation. He was shocked by the reality that surfaced soon after the club was founded. In less than a year, about twenty people showed interest and joined the club: young men and women, Christians, Muslims, students and non-students from across Nigeria. Most of them were scared to come out to family and friends, others had been disowned and driven from home, homeless, needy and hungry. C. Boy was in a fix: money, meeting tuition and housing costs were huge challenges.

I asked how he coped with the situation. He lit a cigarette and thought for a moment before starting to respond.

'Man, it was fucking tough. You know, starting a group, a movement like this one is not like running a political party. It's not a project anyone, including the NGOs here, wants to support. How can you register a group that is already criminalised and demonised even before its emergence? Man, it was fucking tough.' He stopped speaking for another drag, tapped the ash on the ashtray and continued. 'The solace was only in the reality that I could bring troubled people together so they could share their problems in a close but warm space. Survival was a challenge but you know, just as they say, a problem shared is half solved.'

Early in 2014, PBB was able to pay for two flats, in Kaduna and Zaria respectively, for any homeless and troubled member to live in. Both were equipped with studies, computers and Wi-Fi. PBB was able to pay tuition for twenty-three students of its 'parentless' and homeless members in different colleges and universities across Nigeria, and also provide living stipends from all these sources.

Though the main funding for PBB came from C. Boy, the club was able to diversify its sources of funding. Having paid to train some members in photography, film-making, fashion design and app creation, the burden of funding lessened. Almost everyone was a freelance of some kind. More funds came from tickets sales for open mikes, poetry slams, exhibitions and concerts. 'These events are the major strategies through which PBB sends coded signs to society that homosexuals exist here, and are ready to continue existing regardless of any law against them,' C. Boy told me. Most of the artistic outdoor events in Kaduna, Zaria, Jos and Gombe were hosted and managed by PBB's team of concept developers. And of course, strict measures were laid down and followed to keep secret the identities of the people behind the events. 'We are making society feel our energy by curating these events.'

C. Boy chuckled and shook his head when I asked why he wasn't allowing PBB to reach out to foreign organisations sympathetic to the cause of LGBT. 'I don't believe in that bullshit,' he began, rubbing his eyes. He stood up and scurried to the DJ's booth, spoke into the ear of the DJ and returned immediately.

'So sorry for that. Just reminded him to allow time for our brainstorming session. It's important.'

He sat facing me, his back to the dance floor. I looked across his shoulders into the crowd to see if I could find my partner. I didn't see her. It seemed like everyone had found the space and time to dance for the first time in their lives. The music blared, the groove kept on.

I lit another cigarette. C. Boy stared at me with those bored eyes. I reminded him of the question I had asked; he rubbed his eyes again.

He didn't like the idea of foreign aid to Africa in whatever form or guise, particularly 'using Africa as a sympathy tool to benefit from an organised system called "corporate responsibility" '.

'You see, it's so easy to attract sympathy for this kind of cause. Internet and all that, you know,' he said, snapping his finger to show how easy and fast it is to let the world know. 'But the issue is this, we, these guys here, all of us, don't want to be used as ads' contents and objects. I don't want any social media sympathy campaigns, especially those inspired and promoted toward Western organisations. Doing that would be objectifying our dreams, our passions and our bodies. It would be like organised prostitution. It's cheap, and fucking cruel to what we are trying to do.'

'We are learning to stop looking up there (to the West) by working out how we can help ourselves here. How long are we going to keep asking for aid and foreign assistance?' He stopped talking, and reached for his wine.

7

C. Boy told me about his guests – stories defying mainstream narratives about LGBT people in repressive societies like Africa. Stories of pride, ambition and rebellion. There was Musa (not his real name), twenty-three, an Igala Muslim on the dance floor, whose widowed illiterate mother accepted his sexuality; he worked as a studio engineer to support his family. There was Kenny, twenty-seven, a graffiti artist and a born-again Christian who had left home two years ago in search of love. He was hoping for things to improve for gays in Nigeria so he could marry in a church. C. Boy showed me a girl, twenty-two, in a jacket and miniskirt and heels, who was studying biochemistry and working on a book on women, Islam and sexuality in northern Nigeria. She was yet to let any family member know her sexuality. Sitting round a table with friends was Joshua, a married 45-year-old man and a lecturer in a polytechnic. He was the oldest man in the club. C. Boy told me Joshua was preparing a divorce, and hoped to leave the country afterwards. He seemed to be the only one there seeking a new place.

Everyone here recognised the legitimacy of their sexuality. 'We'll be happy knowing this until death comes,' C. Boy said in conclusion. 'And we're glad we know this. Our feelings are legitimate. Fuck whoever thinks otherwise.'

He sipped his drink, heaved the sigh of someone with a lot of things to say, facing huge difficulties saying them.

He lit a cigarette. Instead of smoking it, he held it between his fingers and stared at it glowing and slowly shortening.

8

Depression is so disrespectful, so harassing.

I once confided in a boy when I was at university about my battle with depression since childhood and he gave me this are-you-fucking-serious look. 'Africans don't suffer from depression,' he said. 'It's one of those fashionable things black men say now to sound sophisticated like the white man, like being gay,' he continued, to further undermine the genuineness of my feeling. His opinion broke me down for two reasons. One, the flimsy way humans treat each other. Two, he was a final-year student in social sciences. How could he be so stupid?

11.43 a.m. 11 March 2015, my phone beeped with this text: 'It's here today again. Like never before. Fucking me up like never before. I lost, lost today. Cowardly disappointing. That's me. Sorry!'

It was from C. Boy.

The door was locked from the inside. We broke in. He was nowhere in the room. The windows were flung open. And when we reached the window by his bed and looked down, we saw him. He lay in a pool of coagulated blood on the concrete floor of the backyard. For all these hours he lay there dead with his split-up head, and none of his neighbours knew. He lay there and nobody knew. Death is a solo business anyway. Like depression, it is always a solo transaction. Always.

We called the ambulance. And when we reached his family, they pleaded with us not to reveal to anyone the manner of his death. 'I'm an elder in the church, please protect our name,' his father said on the phone.

The clothes on his bed, floor and chairs seemed like he had contemplated what to put on before climbing out that window and diving off. There were half-closed books on his bed and table, and pencils, dictionaries, notepads, papers, a teacup, ashtray, spoons, erasers, pencil sharpeners, spiral-bound manuscripts, wrapped weed, a Bible, devotional books, unfinished cards of paracetamol and aspirin, bangles and an HP laptop. He had been working on a book, a collection of essays reflecting on Africa's future. 'Dude, this book will shake this continent to its root. Fucking draggy, but I'm called to write this shit. You know, good books always drag,' he said with enthusiasm one night in his flat. He had just returned from seeing his family in Adamawa. Two brothers and a sister and their father. He said he was going to reveal his sexuality to his siblings, and they would be fine with it.

From where I stood in the room I could see a paper pasted on the wall. I walked closer to read the words on it. It read AFRICA'S FUTURE HAS NO SPACE FOR FUCKING STUPID BLACK MEN. *He signed the statement with his name.*

After two weeks in the mortuary, the burial was eventually held on a hot afternoon in Zaria. His siblings and his father didn't show up.

9

About 3 a.m. A dance contest and spoken-word/rap battle were under way. C. Boy suggested we finally rejoin the party. I paused the recording. We moved to the dance floor. And for first time since we came, I saw my partner, in a sweat, on the dance floor, trouncing her challenger.

We are the contestants. In us, Africa finds its true rhythm to contest.

If you stepped in here, you would see all of us – gays, lesbians, bisexuals: oppressed people – refusing to mourn the anti-gay laws. We are making a mockery of it; mourning, for us, is not a virtue. We are reinforcing our passion and existence in this hall, right now, in our own way. Unknown to the world, we are buzzing in here with energy and stamina and dreams. We are laughs. We are smart laughing fires. Our feet are fires; so are our waists, our tongues, our eyes and our passions. You would see us blazing, emitting prophecies. We are fires: smoky hot fires, ready to choke to death the places and imaginations that threaten our survival.

If you were in this hall, you would feel how we assert ourselves through music, words, dance, hair, fashion, technology, ideas and spirits. We are spirits. If you were here, you would notice that we are not the demons roaming your cities and villages with evil and sin in our bosoms. We are not wayward, perverse, queer or funny lovers. We are children of our parents, children of this continent, children of nature, of imagination and of hunger. If you were in this club seeing the tears roll down our eyes, feeling the sweat on our bodies, pouring down our torsos to our pants, as we move to Afrobeat, Afropop, highlife and juju, you would realise that WE ARE CHILDREN OF OUR GODS. We exist.

We are buddies, roomies, comrades; breaking loose from our chains and jumping off the ships, sailing to places where our dreams and our existence would be lynched. We are the holy spirits, and we prefer battling and drowning in fierce oceans and keeping our prophecies safe than to be lynched by foolish black men.

We are children of Africa. And we care to be so.

10

The contests were concluded. We took a break for tea, for cigarettes, for booze, for toilets: for transition. We are the most prominent feature of Africa's transitioning; in us Africa truly rises. Girls headed to the restroom carried handbags, toothbrushes and pullovers. The men seemed not to care; they loitered around, chatting, wine glasses and teacups in hand, wiping off sweat from their bodies, smoking. I grabbed my partner's camera; I snapped anything and anyone I could see. Bottles, shoes, cigarette packs strewn all over the floor; silhouettes of couples smooching around the corners; guys mixing drinks at the bar and yelling at each other; the Afro or dyed or locked or Mohawk or plain hairdos, I snapped them all, the girls returning from the restroom and the boys rearranging the seats. I snapped them. Here, we are the photographs of Africa's budding *pluralities*.

And when we settled down to begin the brainstorming session we all smelled of sweat, booze, cigarettes, confidence and excitement. This is the best part of every party, the time when you don't complain of your neighbour's smell because it's a familiar smell, because it mingles with your own. Smells of mutual experience and lust.

Switching from party mode to intellectual discourse was a drag. Everyone whispered and yawned and chewed and belched: the hangovers from partying. The seats had been rearranged in a circle so we faced one another no matter where we sat. I ran my eyes through to figure our number. We were forty-one. Seventeen girls.

C. Boy and Jenny, the tallest girl and person in the party, launched the session with impassioned speeches.

I continued recording. We were talking about Afro-modernism.

Insights. Theories and counter-theories. Quotations and misquotations, and their debunking and deconstructions. Insults. Anger. Fierceness. Applause. Table banging. Wisdom. Foolishness. Completedness. Unfinishedness. Smelling mouths. Tongues of fire. Energy!

11

Africa is enlarging itself to become a CENTRE too. Africa is coming out to make visible its own CENTRES, headquarters, laboratories and metropolises. Africa is rising. Rising from the centuries-old folly of stupid black people. Africa is de-scribing itself, re-scribing itself and pre-scribing its future; it is reinventing itself through the mouths and imaginations of its babes and sucklings. For out of the mouths of babes and sucklings shall come forth mysteries and inventions and innovations and assertions.

We are babes and sucklings. And our tongues and imaginations are fire.

12

These are the various points and insights from the brainstorming session.

We are neither a theory nor a movement. We are open space: Africa's newest genre. We are the *unemployables*, dissidents, techies, pan-Africanists, designers, etc., coming out, in the twenty-first century, in our different corners, to challenge the centuries-old notion that *Africa does little thinking, trades badly and is even worse at buying.*

'Afro-moderns do nothing but look at and in and with and for Africa and its future, with the hope of reinventing and re-energising it,' Baban Gida says. 'We are economists, industrialists and investors renegotiating Africa's trade terms and conditions. We are not white-collar aspirants or mere civil servants or lame creatives. Afro-modernism makes the case to stretch "all of this" continent to the space where it becomes the centre of the world.' He concludes his point to thunderous applause and yells.

Afro-moderns are renegotiating and/or terminating the skewed contracts, contracts signed by our forefathers and their stupid descendants in power who are still ruining the continent today.

Afro-moderns know how badly their stupid forefathers performed in the past and are now refusing to mourn it. They know about colonialism and slavery and neocolonialism and imperialism and other isms unfavourable to Africa, but are not going to keep wailing over the deeds and greed of devilish, vile, horrendous and criminal white people like those idiotic postcolonial scholars did, the people who squandered a precious chance, before and after independence, to create a true continent. Afro-moderns are neither Afro-romantics nor Negritudes. They are not critics and insulters of white people, or the other kinds of crap.

Afro-moderns are interested in a non-romantic view of Africa. That's how they hope to see it, and thereby recreate it. That's how to create its new curricula, its new politics, its new arts and aesthetics, its new business, its new industry, its pluralities.

Afro-moderns are men and women whose only family, industry and business is Africa. And the constant pursuit is to expand, diversify, energise, imagine and reimagine it. We are farmers, engineers, artists, technocrats, industrialists, scientists, negotiators; professionals living and working for Africa with the sole aim of growing, raising and branding it. We are homosexuals, heterosexuals, bisexuals, transexuals and whateversexuals burning to rescue this continent from the ruins of stupid black men. We are not only the turning-point generation; we are also Africa's hugest turning, biggest point and boldest generation.

13

Ishaku, twenty-four, was on his feet describing what he preferred Afro-modernism to be known as when one of the bouncers walked in to C. Boy and whispered something in his ear. They left for the door together, speaking in a low voice.

It wasn't long. C. Boy hurried back into the hall, to the DJ's booth and pulled out a bag. He put something that I didn't see in his back pocket and walked back to the door. He looked troubled.

It was 4.15 a.m. Something was wrong.

One by one, everyone moved to the door.

We heard sirens blaring at a distance, approaching the club. There was a push at the door. A scamper, as everyone ran back to the hall. No one seemed to know what it was exactly, but the word 'police' was on everyone's lips. 'They've come for us. We are busted,' someone, I don't remember who, said.

The sirens were outside. Someone gave C. Boy a hard push from the door and he fell backwards into the hall. He quickly stood back on his feet, as seven masked policemen, armed with guns, walked inside. There was a huge silence. Another officer, without a mask or a gun, walked in after his men. The officers began searching the DJ's booth, the restrooms, the bar and the dark corners here and there. It took ten to fifteen minutes.

They returned and, guns pointing, asked all of us to sit on the floor. We sat. Nobody dared to speak.

'Who's Marshal here? Marshal Dominic?' the officer asked no one in particular.

There was no one. No Marshal here.

'No one here goes by that name.' It was Joshua speaking.

At this time, one of the policemen located a light switch to the brighter lights in the club and turned them on. The club's laser lights were too weak to make out people's faces. The officer had a photograph in his hand; he started moving from person to person, comparing their faces to the picture. He walked round and didn't find a match.

He came back to where he first stood, and nodded to the policemen to move to the door. It was tense. I felt a pain in my chest. Everyone stared at him with eyes that spoke of fear of lynching or imprisonment.

He looked at the photograph again before bringing his eyes to us, searching. Then he cleared his throat. 'This guy is a murderer and we got tipped he would be here this night. He clubs here.' He moved closer to us, raised the photograph for us to see. 'Anyone seen this guy?'

We shook our heads.

He walked out. They walked out. The sirens started again. And they left.

Fear dehumanises.

Fear of being caught as gay in Nigeria demeans one's humanity. Fear of Nigeria's police arresting you for being homosexual crushes every gut you have.

Jenny burst out crying. Joshua rushed to her, put his hand round her and started crying too. Leila joined in, Kenny was groaning, and my partner walked up to me and let out a loud cry. Then everyone began crying as if we had just turned orphans.

Tears taste like salt. Our tears. We are salts. Africa's salt. And we are here shedding tears because we are trampled upon on every side. But these men don't know this: that the more they trample upon us, the tastier we become.

Musa stood up, started for the restroom. As he turned to the door, he fell down. A heavy crash. We rushed to him. He was having a fit, the fiercest convulsion I have seen all my life. His hands and legs shook turbulently, like they had a life of their own.

There was commotion. We ran back and forth, with water from the restroom. We pulled off our clothes and fanned him with them. I ran outside, and our friend with the car was there waiting. I ran back in, and we carried him into the car. Joshua and Kenny sat in the back and we laid him on their legs. My partner sat in front. They drove off to the hospital.

It was 5.13 a.m.

Everyone sat about in the hall, fatigued and broken. C. Boy sat on the seat by the check-in. I joined him. We sat in silence.

I lit a cigarette and gave it to him. He refused.

'Look at the boy, the poor boy. Did you see him?' He started talking, his voice nearing a cry. 'What had he done to be frightened in that way? For being something else?' I didn't answer.

'We may have ended this event on a bad note, but I tell you we've made a huge statement. We've started something.' He brought out a revolver from his back pocket and kept it on the table.

'I can't close my eyes and let anyone hurt any of these people. I can't. Dude, I can't.'

We sat in silence. A few people started to leave the club.

'I need to go,' I said. C. Boy didn't respond. He stared down. I walked to the bar for water, and when I returned he was no longer sitting. He was on the floor, crying and asking, 'What have we done to be scared to death like that? What did that small boy do to deserve such a scare? What?'

I didn't answer. If I did, tears would start running from my eyes. So, I just stood and watched this 27-year-old man sitting on the floor and weeping because he was homosexual. I didn't answer.

14

Boy, that night was energy. The night I last saw C. Boy.

Suicide is a means of taking flight to hibernate too, a means of kinetic energy too.

Fuck whoever thinks otherwise. ∎

Sylvia Legris

The Heart Compared to a Seed, c.1508 (after Leonardo da Vinci)

Through The Long Clearing, through The Cutting, through
The Stick-Stockade. Through Valley of the Chain-Link,
through Blind-Ditch, through Field of Flowers.

Through Charcoal-Burner's Place, through Little-Market
Bridge, through Well Woods. Through Marble Spring,
Swamp Spring, Cold Spring.

. . . Broadcast the heart.

Seed the double-sided sheet. Verso: the River of Inky Liver
and Spleen, the Sprung from the Earth Kidneys bleeding
through—the tortuous hoary vessels. Seed Long Hill and
Mountain Hill, Pigeon Hill and Cat Hill. Seed mulberry,
cedar, the hardened softwooded arteries.

Seed the Sovereign Tree, seed the Tree of Inevitable Strife,
cultivate the evident. Recto: The Principal Organ (give
Aristotle his Pride of Place); the core—*nocciolo*;

noce, the heart—the nut that gestates the tree of veins.

NOTE ON THE POEM: The names listed are Renaissance place names of one
region of central Italy.

CONTRIBUTORS

Suzanne Brøgger is the author of more than twenty works of fiction, essays and memoir, including the autobiographical trilogy of liberation, experimentation and identity, *Crème Fraiche*, *Yes* and *Transparence*. She has been a member of the Danish Academy since 1997.

Vahni Capildeo is a British Trinidadian writer. Her work includes *Measures of Expatriation*, shortlisted for the T.S. Eliot Prize, and *Utter*, which speaks from her experience as an Oxford English Dictionary lexicographer. She is travelling to the Caribbean and East Africa, on a Harper-Wood Studentship, to write about natural and cultivated environments.

Emma Cline is the author of *The Girls* and the winner of the *Paris Review* Plimpton Prize in 2014.

Kathleen Collins was a pioneer African-American playwright, film-maker, civil rights activist and educator. Her film, *Losing Ground*, is a portrayal of a black female intellectual. Collins died in 1988 at the age of forty-six.

Pwaangulongii Dauod is the former creative director at Ilmihouse – an art house in Kaduna, Nigeria – and is a 2016 MacDowell Colony fellow. He is currently working on two books, a collection of essays, *Africa's Future Has No Space for Stupid Black Men*, and a story collection, *The Uses of Unhappiness*.

Steven Dunn is the author of *Potted Meat*, forthcoming from Tarpaulin Sky Press. He was born and raised in West Virginia, and after spending ten years in the US Navy, earned a BA in Creative Writing from the University of Denver. He is Reviews and Interviews Editor for *Horse Less Press*.

Patrick Flanery was born and raised in the US and now lives in London. He is the author of the novels *Absolution*, *Fallen Land* and, most recently, *I Am No One*.

Claire Hajaj is a journalist of mixed Jewish-Palestinian heritage and the author of *Ishmael's Oranges*. She has worked in the Middle East and other conflict zones alongside humanitarian workers and UN peacebuilding missions. She lives in Beirut.

Joanna Kavenna is the author of several books, including *The Ice Museum*, *Inglorious* (which won the Orange Award for New Writers), *The Birth of Love* and *Tomorrow*. Her writing has appeared in the *New Yorker*, the *Guardian*, the *London Review of Books*, the *New York Times* and other publications. In 2013, she was selected as one of *Granta*'s Best of Young British Novelists. Her next novel will be *A Field Guide to Reality*, forthcoming by Quercus.

Melissa Lee-Houghton is a poet, fiction writer and essayist, named one of the Next Generation Poets by the Poetry Book Society in 2014. Her latest poetry collection, *Sunshine*, and the book, *An Insight into Mental Health in Britain – Five Essays*, will be published in 2016.

Sylvia Legris's next book of poems, *The Hideous Hidden*, is forthcoming in 2016. Her collection, *Pneumatic Antiphonal*, was published as part of the New Directions Poetry Pamphlets series. Her third book, *Nerve Squall*, won the 2006 Griffin Poetry Prize. Originally from Winnipeg, she lives in Saskatoon, Canada.

Victor Lodato is an author and playwright. His novel, *Mathilda Savitch*, won the PEN USA Award for Fiction. His stories and essays have appeared in the *New Yorker*, the *New York Times* and *The Best American Short Stories*. His new novel, *Edgar and Lucy*, will be published in March 2017.

Hoa Nguyen was born in the Mekong Delta and raised in the Washington, DC area. Her poetry collections include *As Long As Trees Last*, *Red Juice* and *Violet Energy Ingots*, which is forthcoming from Wave Books. She lives in Toronto.

Gwendoline Riley's 'First Love' is taken from her new novel of the same title, forthcoming from Granta Books in the UK and Melville House in the US in 2017. She is the author of four other novels, and has won the Betty Trask Prize, the Somerset Maugham Award and been shortlisted for the John Llewllyn Rhys Prize.

Jacob Aue Sobol is a Danish photographer. After studying at the European Film College, he was admitted to Fatamorgana, the Danish School of Art Photography. He has lived in Canada, Greenland and Japan. *Sabine* was nominated for the 2005 Deutsche Börse Photography Prize.

GRANTA
THE MAGAZINE OF NEW WRITING

PRINT SUBSCRIPTION REPLY FORM FOR US, CANADA
AND LATIN AMERICA (includes digital and app access).
For digital-only subscriptions, please visit granta.com/subscriptions.

GUARANTEE: If I am ever dissatisfied with my *Granta* subscription, I will simply notify you, and
you will send me a complete refund or credit my credit card, as applicable, for all un-mailed issues.

YOUR DETAILS

TITLE ....

NAME ....

ADDRESS ....

....

CITY.. STATE ....

ZIP CODE .... COUNTRY ....

EMAIL ....

☐ Please check this box if you do not wish to receive special offers from *Granta*
☐ Please check this box if you do not wish to receive offers from organisations selected
by *Granta*

PAYMENT DETAILS

1 year subscription: ☐ US: $48 ☐ Canada: $56 ☐ Latin America: $68

3 year subscription: ☐ US: $120 ☐ Canada: $144 ☐ Latin America: $180

Enclosed is my check for $ _____ made payable to *Granta*.

Please charge my: ☐ Visa ☐ MasterCard ☐ Amex

Card No. ☐☐☐☐☐☐☐☐☐☐☐☐☐☐☐☐

Expiration date ☐☐ / ☐☐

Security Code ☐☐☐☐☐

SIGNATURE .... DATE ....

Please mail this order form with your payment instructions to:

Granta Publications
PO Box 359
Congers, NY 10920-0359

Or call 845-267-3031
Or visit GRANTA.COM/SUBSCRIPTIONS for details

Source code: BUS135PM